A Concise Guide to
Technical Communication

A Concise
Guide to Technical
Communication

HEATHER GRAVES & ROGER GRAVES

broadview press

BROADVIEW PRESS – www.broadviewpress.com
Peterborough, Ontario, Canada

Founded in 1985, Broadview Press remains a wholly independent publishing house. Broadview's focus is on academic publishing; our titles are accessible to university and college students as well as scholars and general readers. With 800 titles in print, Broadview has become a leading international publisher in the humanities, with world-wide distribution. Broadview is committed to environmentally responsible publishing and fair business practices.

Library and Archives Canada Cataloguing in Publication

Title: A concise guide to technical communication / Heather Graves & Roger Graves.
Names: Graves, Heather, 1958- author. | Graves, Roger, 1957- author.
Description: Includes bibliographical references and index.
Identifiers: Canadiana (print) 20200290398 | Canadiana (ebook) 20200290460 | ISBN 9781554815487 (softcover) | ISBN 9781770487604 (PDF) | ISBN 9781460407141 (EPUB)
Subjects: LCSH: Technical writing. | LCSH: Communication of technical information.
Classification: LCC T11 .G747 2020 | DDC 808.06/66—dc23

Broadview Press handles its own distribution in North America:
PO Box 1243, Peterborough, Ontario K9J 7H5, Canada
555 Riverwalk Parkway, Tonawanda, NY 14150, USA
Tel: (705) 743-8990; Fax: (705) 743-8353
email: customerservice@broadviewpress.com

For all territories outside of North America, distribution is handled by Eurospan Group.

 Broadview Press acknowledges the financial support of the Government of Canada for our publishing activities.

Edited by Tania Therien
Book Design by Em Dash Design

PRINTED IN CANADA

Contents

Preface

NOTE TO INSTRUCTORS

First, thank you for selecting the *Concise Guide to Technical Communication* as your course text. The *Concise Guide* offers a concise but comprehensive introduction of strategies for your students that will help them create effective technical documents and presentations. This book does not follow the standard organization of many texts with the theory and conceptual information in the chapters and then a variety of exercises and assignments collected at the end. Instead, the exercises and assignments are placed within the chapters, following the discussion of the relevant concepts or points. The idea is that students should read the chapter prior to class and, when they get to class, you can quickly summarize for them the main points to which they should pay attention. Then you can assign an exercise that will reinforce the theoretical concept and get students started working with it. Theoretical discussions about writing are useful, to a point, but they really become relevant when the ideas are applied to a particular text or situation. The exercises embedded in the chapter serve to show students how the ideas may immediately and usefully be applied to their own situations.

There are several different kinds of exercises and assignments in the book. **IN-CLASS EXERCISES** are short assignments intended to be done by students in class in 15 or 20 minutes. They ask students to use the main ideas discussed in the previous section and to think critically about those ideas. Sometimes, the exercises complicate a simplistic view of writing; other times, they have students become comfortable with a strategy that they will need to use in a longer, more formal assignment later in the class or term. **LAB ASSIGNMENTS** are slightly longer than in-class exercises, but they are still intended to be completed (or at least worked on) during a class meeting. For instructors who book a computer lab for some or all of their class meetings, these assignments get students working with the central principles covered in this book. If you do not use or do not have access to a computer lab for your technical communication class, the lab assignments are still useful for helping students apply the writing strategies. The assignments may be finished and handed in at the end of class, or they may be taken home and finished before the next class. Students can bring the finished version to the next class meeting or email it to you, depending upon your preference. The third type of assignment is the **MAJOR PROJECT**, which is a longer, more formal assignment that has students consider the main concepts from the chapter (or chapters) to produce an effective example of one of the main genres of technical communication. Assign the major project at the beginning of a particular unit of study and have it due the following week or at the end of the term, depending upon your course plan and schedule.

Consider having your students work collaboratively on the in-class and the lab assignments. Because much technical communication is written collaboratively, these group activities further learning through opportunities to work with others, to discuss the course content, and to hear others' bright ideas that might spark greater creativity overall. Group activities also allow students to get to know each other in ways that promote a positive learning environment. Collaborative work generally results in better written texts and less grading time because the in-class and lab assignments result in 6 or 7 papers for quick review rather than 25 or 30 individual efforts. We do recommend limiting the groups for in-class work to a maximum of four people because larger groups mean that some contribute little to the activity. Two or three to a group is an ideal size to form a productive unit. We have also used the major projects as collaborative assignments with good success. If you decide to do so, limit the size of the group to three people. We do not expand the requirements for collaborative projects, nor do we grade the collaborative assignments harder. We find that negotiating the group dynamics is an excellent additional lesson for students, and the finished project can provide them with evidence for future employers that they work effectively with others. The advantage to you is that you have fewer final projects to grade during the last weeks of the term.

Depending upon your course goals and your term length, you may decide to cover the chapters in the order in which they are presented in this text. Do not feel that you have to, however. With the demands of a short term—in some cases a ten-week quarter—you can use the chapters in the order that suits your students' needs and the assignment schedule.

Although this volume contains ten chapters, several chapters contain information that may take you longer than a week to cover in class. For example, Chapter 7 contains discussions about status or progress reports, white papers, and recommendation reports. You could easily spend a week on each of these genres if you wished to focus your technical communication course on reports. Similarly, Chapter 4, "Writing Technical Prose," could be assigned at least two weeks. In fact, you could easily spend three or four class meetings on discussions of style and the use of definition and description in technical prose.

Similarly, you can spend several weeks covering the information in most chapters since students benefit greatly from opportunities to develop their technical communication skills, as well as interviewing or surveying skills through multiple chances to try out the strategies and revise their efforts. Students benefit from chances to work with others while they learn how to practise the conventions for creating effective visuals. We have found that hands-on exercises in the computer lab help students to learn a great deal in a short time; they can interact with each other and experiment with new techniques while having the instructor present to give quick feedback or help them out with a tip or shortcut. We have also found that students can teach us (and each other) many tips and shortcuts for using technology.

NOTE TO STUDENTS

First, thank you for purchasing this book. It should provide you with ideas and strategies to help you create effective technical documents. This book takes a rhetorical approach to technical communication. This means that instead of setting up a list of rules that you should apply uniformly to all writing situations, this book introduces you to the bigger picture of how the words you write can affect the people intended to use them. By understanding who your readers or users are and what they need in a technical document, you can adapt your knowledge to their situations to provide them with what they need. This book should help you do this by outlining some specific strategies, demonstrating ways that they might be used, and summarizing the challenges that certain documents or genres present. The exercises and assignments in each chapter will help you practise the strategies and apply the concepts that you need to make good decisions about how to write a document, and they will guide you in developing a good working draft. When you test your document with members of your target user group, you should receive feedback that will help you revise the draft into a usable piece of work. Since the key to good technical communication is to provide the information that target users need, we can measure the success of a document by the productive experience users have with it. Your goal, as a writer of technical documents, should be to present usable information on a specialized (and usually technical) subject matter to readers or users who lack knowledge in that area. If you are not already an expert in the area or subject that you need to write about, your first task is to learn enough about it so that you can direct the learning and experience of others. This book will help you figure out how to educate yourself as well as facilitate the learning of others.

ACKNOWLEDGMENTS

First, we have to thank the hundreds (maybe thousands) of students whom we have taught at Illinois State University, DePaul University in Chicago, Western University in London, Ontario, and the University of Alberta for motivating us to develop the teaching materials that form the basis for this book. The students at DePaul University were especially helpful because they refused to just talk about technical communication but insisted on doing it and on learning ways to do it well. These demands forced us to take a concise but also strategic approach to teaching technical communication, to developing specific strategies that improve the organization of documents, that create a compelling and well-supported argument, and these strategies are laid out in this text. We also appreciate the generosity of the numerous students who gave us permission to reproduce their work in this book. We felt it was important to include examples of what students enrolled in a technical writing course at college and university levels could reasonably be expected to achieve in response to the assignments in this text. We could not have met this objective without our students' support and enthusiasm.

We would also like to thank the various instructors who have used earlier versions of this book and given us feedback that has improved this draft. These instructors include Chris Tardy at the University of Arizona, Ethan Sproat at Utah Valley University, and Jo-Anne Andre and Doug Brent at the University of Calgary.

We would also like to thank Marjorie Mather for proposing that we create a *Concise Guide*. Thanks also to the board of directors at Broadview Press, for supporting this new book. We also want to thank the reviewers who gave us valuable suggestions at both the proposal and manuscript stages of the process. With their feedback, we were able to make some significant changes and additions to the book to make it more useful. We would also like to thank Tara Lowes for her effort and time producing this book and Tara Trueman for shepherding the manuscript through the production process. We are also indebted to Tania Therien for her careful and respectful editing of the manuscript. We especially appreciate how tactfully she corrected our unclear and sometimes infelicitous phrasing. Thanks also to Michel Pharand who proofread with great care to help to make the final version as clear and error-free as possible. Thank you to Matthew Jubb who did a wonderful job choosing the fonts and designing the interior. We also wish to thank Erich Mulhall and Stacey Aspinall for their excellent work putting together a terrific website to support this project. Finally, thanks also to our children, Erin and Eric.

Heather Graves
Roger Graves
wecanwrite.ca
@rogergraves (Twitter)
roger@wecanwrite.ca

CHAPTER ONE

Audience, Purpose, Genre, and Medium

WHAT IS TECHNICAL COMMUNICATION?

Technical communication refers to the activity of preparing and publishing specialized information in a way that allows non-specialists to understand and use the information to accomplish some task. While the information can be presented verbally in an oral presentation, a class, or even over the phone, it most often takes a written or visual form. Although it was founded relatively recently (in 2005), YouTube® has become a main outlet for video of all kinds. Over one billion people use YouTube—one out of every two Internet users. Today's technical communicators have YouTube and many other online mediums for delivering content. Effective technical communication in 2020 demands multimedia approaches to communication, an understanding and ability to use social media, and fundamental rhetorical awareness of who you are communicating with (audience), what you are trying to communicate (message), why you are trying to communicate this message to this audience (purpose), how you propose to get the message across (genre), and what medium will best accomplish your purpose.

Here are some examples of technical communication:

- online manuals (print or PDF versions as well as help screens)
- assembly instructions for appliances, equipment, furniture, toys, and games
- research articles that present scientific or technological discoveries
- magazine articles that explain how to complete a process—preparing yellow chicken curry or a dovetail joint
- training videos that demonstrate a process
- instructions on how to register online or create an online account
- online communities of users that exchange and/or continuously update technical information or document processes

In most cases, readers of technical communication come to the information to learn or to do something that otherwise they could not do. If effective, the technical communication should make it possible—and even easy—to comprehend the information and to act on it to perform the task. Technical documents generally share this main purpose: to inform.

HOW DOES TECHNICAL COMMUNICATION DIFFER FROM OTHER TYPES OF COMMUNICATION?

All writing takes place in a specific context, and all writing involves these elements: a writer/speaker, a message, and a reader/listener. Two of the main differences between technical communication and other types of communication are that 1) its subject matter usually requires some type of specialized knowledge and 2) it provides a bridge for the non-specialist reader to complete an action successfully. It also incorporates visual elements where they help readers more easily accomplish the task. Some people call technical communication "instrumental" because it works as an instrument or tool for people to get something done.

Figure 1.1 shows one way to think about the relationship between writer, reader, and text in any kind of writing. In this diagram, reality forms a third point on the triangle, which shapes the relationship between the writer (encoder), the reader (decoder), and the text or document (signal). In technical communication, the text represents a version of reality prepared by the writer for the reader. Each type of writing focuses on a different aspect of the triangle. For example, writing that focuses on the writer/speaker is called "expressive," and examples include personal letters, diaries, and journals. Writing that focuses on the reader/listener is called "persuasive," and examples include advertising and editorials in newspapers. Writing with a central focus on the text itself (the words) is "literary"; examples include the kinds of literature studied in English classes: poetry, fiction, and drama. Finally, writing that focuses on "reality" is technical and scientific and includes textbooks, user instructions, and reports.

One major flaw in this model is the omission of context. We could add it to the model as a rectangle around the triangle. While important in any writing, context is crucial in technical and professional communication because it affects how users understand texts. Ignoring context guarantees that your writing is unsuccessful: for example, you might create a short instructional video for operating a chainsaw but the operators' context for viewing the video is outdoors with no place to set the device down and, and when the chainsaw is running, an environment too loud to hear any voiceover. A rectangular card, laminated in plastic, is a more usable format for this instructional information, one that recognizes the context for its use by the chainsaw operator and responds to this need.

How can the communication triangle help you to evaluate the writing situation for particular documents? Gather and analyze some sample documents to find out. Focus on aspects that make it easier to think about the different angles of the communication situation as well as on those features that the triangle does *not* allow you to think about.

A second drawback to the communication triangle is that it encourages us to think that these different angles (writer, reader, text, and reality) are separate—that, for example, newspaper reports describe reality but do not try to persuade

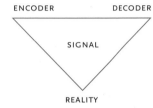

FIGURE 1.1

Kinneavy's communication triangle.

Source: James L. Kinneavy, A Theory of Discourse *(New York: Norton, 1971), 61. Reprinted with permission.*

FIGURE 1.2

Beale's model of communication.

Source: Walter H. Beale, A Pragmatic Theory of Rhetoric *(Carbondale: Southern Illinois UP, 1987), 114. Reprinted with permission.*

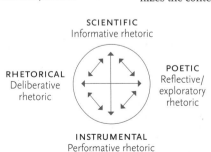

readers to adopt a perspective on the topic. The point is that rhetorical genres often—maybe always—overlap. A better way to show this overlapping is demonstrated in Figure 1.2.

You will notice that Beale's categories for writing differ from those of the communication triangle. He discusses the purpose or aim of different types of writing. He focuses on aim to highlight the relationships created between the writer, the reader, reality, and the text in each type of writing. For example, poetic writing (or discourse) relates to the writer and enables the writer's self-expression or self-exploration. Readers read poetic (or literary) discourse to explore writers' personal visions. In contrast, writers of instrumental discourse link readers and reality: they provide information to help readers perform a particular action. This type of document becomes a tool to accomplish an action. Writers of rhetorical discourse aim to persuade readers—to change their minds about a particular issue or belief (or at least prompt them to consider the writer's viewpoint, even briefly). And, finally, writers of scientific discourse seek to relate readers to reality differently from writers of instrumental discourse, by informing and educating readers about complex technical ideas.

Notice the arrows on Beale's diagram: they indicate that a text—a newspaper report, for example—can sometimes have dual aims. It may *inform* you about some event while also trying to *persuade* you to condemn or applaud those events. In fact, some people argue that it is impossible for a piece of writing to have only one function. This view raises the possibility that every piece of writing does double work. For example, as a consumer, when you compare the assembly instructions for two different brands of bookshelves, you may decide to buy the one that presents the process as easy and pleasant (a persuasive goal) as well as clearly showing you how to do it (the instrumental goal). The instructions may start with a paragraph that describes the innovative features of the bookshelf design (informational and persuasive goals), while also including a list of tools you need for the assembly (an informational goal). How many different types of goals can you identify in several different writing samples?

NOTE ON CREATIVE VS. TECHNICAL WRITING

Many people who don't know much about technical communication beyond their experience as a user struggling with poorly written assembly instructions or a badly organized appliance manual view technical communication as dull and uninspiring. When asked about it, they often contrast technical writing with creative or fiction writing. They think of the latter category as innovative, imaginative, and artistic, while they consider technical writing to be dry and unimaginative. And poorly done technical

---

IN-CLASS EXERCISE 1.1

Applying the Communication Triangle to Sample Documents

Assemble a collection of documents, some that are examples of technical communication and others that are examples of professional or business communication. For example, here is a selection of possible documents:

- the user's manual for an appliance such as a toaster oven
- a flier that arrived in your junk mail recently
- the installation guide that came with the mini-blinds (or other DIY product)
- a brochure that you picked up in the grocery store or the doctor's office
- a letter from a non-profit organization asking for donations
- the bill from your phone

Now, analyze your collection of documents individually from the perspective of the communication triangle:

- Who is the writer?
- Who is the intended reader?
- What are the purposes of the document?
- What form does the document take?
- In what way does the content of the document represent reality?
- What characteristics do these documents share?
- What limitations do you see to the communication triangle as you seek to apply it to the selection of documents that you collected?

IN-CLASS EXERCISE 1.2

Analyzing Documents with Multiple Aims

Assemble a second collection of documents that includes a broader range of sample documents: add a short story or poem; a newspaper article; a magazine article; a set of instructions; a business letter or two; some advertising fliers or brochures; a scientific report, if you have one; a magazine or newspaper editorial; a business form, questionnaire, or bill. Study these different types of documents from the perspective of Beale's model, illustrated in Figure 1.2.

- What is the main purpose or aim (i.e., rhetorical, scientific, poetic, or instrumental) of the document?
- What kinds of secondary aims does it have?
- Which other categories might it also fit well into?
- How easy is it to assign a primary category to each document?
- What kinds of documents make it difficult to determine a primary aim or purpose?

writing can be all of these negatives—and more. But effective technical communication can be innovative, imaginative, artistic—in a word: creative.

Often, technical writers get to use a product before anyone else, and they are challenged with the job of creating documentation that enables others to use this product quickly and easily. The writer decides on a useful format and medium; figures out how best to illustrate the product, when visuals would be helpful; designs a page layout that will make the process or the product attractive and easy to use; and produces text that is clear, unambiguous, and easy to read. While producing such prose is not usually introspective, the way that journal or novel writing might be, it is still an intriguing and creative process, a process that will change people's lives in small but significant ways. When users understand the basics of how to use a machine or computer program, they can move toward greater skill and more opportunities to take on new challenges. The technical writer becomes a partner in this process, helping users to develop and improve their knowledge and skill.

MEDIUM: WHEN DOES THE MEDIUM USED FOR COMMUNICATION CHANGE IT SUBSTANTIALLY?

Recent work on theories of how documents fulfill communicative goals sees each document as part of a network of related documents, people, and systems. Spinuzzi argues that the meaning of a particular document—and the purpose it serves—depends on its relationship with other documents already in the

FIGURE 1.3
The network as model of communication contexts.

network and on how various networks circulate knowledge and information.[1] Johnson-Eilola suggests that the image of a datacloud captures the complexity, depth, and obscurity of the systems we use to exchange information online.[2] Figure 1.3 suggests how documents, people, and networks (physical and social) all combine to create the context for today's technical communications. One way to think about this is to consider the interactions between documents reviewing a new song posted to a band's website; the reviews of that song on various social media websites; and information about the song on a radio station website. Some even argue that the reputation or value of the song or document rests more with the online commentary of users/listeners than with the intentions of the author of a technical communication document. Swarts argues that the role of the technical communicator should now focus on how to coordinate and cultivate user communities that themselves generate knowledge, processes, and strategies for other users.[3]

1 Clay Spinuzzi, *Network: Theorizing Knowledge Work in Telecommunications* (Cambridge: Cambridge University Press, 2008).

2 Johndan Johnson-Eilola, *Datacloud: Toward a New Theory of Online Work* (Creskill, NJ: Hampton Press, 2005).

3 Jason Swarts, *Wicked, Incomplete, and Uncertain: User Support in the Wild and the Role of Technical Communication* (Logan: Utah State University Press, 2018).

AUDIENCE

WHO USES TECHNICAL COMMUNICATIONS?

In technical communication, it is more accurate to think of your reader as a "user" rather than as a member of a live audience. Originally, "audience" was a metaphor, taken from theatre and referring to the people who observe a performance. Today's viewers of online videos can leave comments, "like" videos, and rate them as ways to provide feedback. Similar feedback opportunities occur on ecommerce sites and on sites that provide recommendations for restaurants and various services. Today, most online help systems ask for this kind of feedback. Users are active participants in the performance of the technical communication text: they have become much closer to the actors' role than the audience's role because they make the writer's words live by using them to do something, instead of just passively observing. If you think of your readers as an audience at all, think of them as a raucous one.

Technical communication users are also very different from the types of readers you will address for school-related assignments. Professors and instructors in post-secondary education dutifully read every word that you write. Not so in the workplace. In fact, much of the text that you write in the workplace will be skimmed, not read, because readers' goals are different. Teachers read to evaluate the quality of the prose and the insightfulness of the ideas. While workplace readers may also evaluate these elements in passing, these readers are far more focused on other concerns as they interact with your document—for example, how to accomplish a task, where to locate information necessary to make a decision, or how to identify potential solutions to a problem. In fact, the parts of a technical report in the workplace

IN-CLASS EXERCISE 1.3

Analyzing Online Communications

Assemble a third collection of documents, this time drawn from online sources. Include user reviews from websites, questions and responses from online help communities, and website documents that also exist as PDF print documents. Examine the online context for these communications.

- Who answers questions that users pose in a forum?
- Is the forum moderated?
- How does the forum indicate or mark expert respondents?
- Do the PDF documents replicate the audience and power relationships of the print documents?
- Are the PDF documents referred to in the forums?
- What role do visuals and/or videos play in online contexts?
- When do videos assume priority or prime responsibility for communication, and when do they play a secondary role?

that receive the most focused reader attention include the executive summary (a summary of the key points in the report), the introduction, and the conclusion. Even these parts are generally skimmed rather than read closely. The body of the report often receives fractionally more attention than the appendices of a report. Because they are often glanced over rather than read closely, technical documents work most effectively when they present information in ways that aid skimming, for example, the use of bulleted lists; the repetition of key ideas (in the letter of transmittal, the summary, the conclusions); or the use of bold or colored typefaces to highlight key points. While no one may pore over your texts in the workplace the way that they do in post-secondary institutions, you are still expected to put extensive effort and care into all aspects of the technical documentation you create. Readers in the workplace will judge your competency and intelligence based on their perceived professionalism of the documents that you produce as part of your employment.

Another way in which readers or users of technical communication differ from the audience for other types of writing is that they are rarely "general," as in a "general audience." In fact, technical communication that addresses a "general audience" is usually poor writing, poor because it assumes that all users have the same level of knowledge about the subject matter, the same background and experience, the same attitude toward the information that they are learning, and so on. One way to visualize the critical differences among users of technical communication is to imagine yourself as a new employee for a roofing company. If you have never laid shingles before, on your first day of work when a co-worker points out to you that the first layer of shingles must be laid backwards—that is, with the unnotched edge laid parallel to the edge of the roof—you will be relieved and grateful to hear this tip. However, after you have been roofing for several months, such a "tip" will irritate you because you have laid the first row many times. Such basic information was essential when you were a novice roofer; it is unnecessary when you are an experienced roofer.

The same situation applies in technical communication: experienced or advanced users reject instructions that provide information that they already know. They do not want to sift through material to find nuggets of new information. Similarly, first-time users become frustrated and angry with instructions that omit the most basic steps—for example, to hit the enter key after selecting a particular command. They lack the experience to add the step that is obvious to everyone else. Users' needs vary widely, making broadly targeted technical documentation of limited use to everyone. The challenge for technical writers becomes finding ways to help users sort through information to find what they are looking for.

WAYS OF THINKING ABOUT USERS

Before we consider specific users, here are some ways to think about how to group users. For example, if you are writing a users' guide on how to create cascading style sheets in Adobe® Creative Suite® software, think about who might open this guide and why. Obviously, anyone who owns a copy of Dreamweaver® and who wants to create a cascading style sheet would use this guide. And this kind of person could very likely be your **PRIMARY AUDIENCE**— that is, the group of users that you expect to choose your guide to create the style sheet. Your primary audience is the major group of users who will use your instructions. To create the style sheet, they will fulfill your purpose in creating the guide—to show somewhat experienced users of Dreamweaver how to use this advanced function.

Is this the only group who may use your guide? Actually, there are other users who also may consult your guide. For example, someone who has created style sheets in the past but may not have done so in several months: this user might open your guide to refresh their memory on getting started. Rather than following step-by-step through your instructions, he or she may skim the guide, noting forgotten details. This user—an expert—will form a **SECONDARY AUDIENCE** for the guide when using it as a reference, not a how-to document. These secondary users have a different level of knowledge than do your primary users, but they may still consult your guide.

Three other groups may also use or affect the use of your guide. When you are first assigned the project, your boss (or, in class, your instructor) becomes an **INITIAL AUDIENCE**—the individual who will approve your project, affecting whether or not your guide reaches the primary audience. A fourth group that may affect whether your project reaches its primary user is the **GATEKEEPER AUDIENCE**. This individual is often a supervisor higher up in the organization who will give final approval on your guide, that is, decide whether to publish it. The gatekeeper audience might give feedback about how the guide should contribute to the organization's image, feedback that could result in revisions to its style or arrangement. This supervisor may shape the document without using it or learning the process that you teach.

A fifth group that could affect your document is the **WATCHDOG AUDIENCE**. The watchdog audience might be a government or regulatory organization unconnected with you directly but that reviews the products that your organization creates. This type of audience may not have the power to prevent or promote publication of your guide, but its members' comments may affect your employer's reputation. For example, your guide may fit its target audience well; reviewers might post glowing reviews about your guide on amazon.com or indigo.ca, resulting in dramatic increases in sales and attention and imitation from other technical writers. Through its evaluation and approval, this watchdog audience might propel your guide to the new industry standard.

While you may have to negotiate through the initial and gatekeeper audiences as you develop your guide, the main group that will shape its details and organization will be your primary users. Their background knowledge and expertise will drive your design decisions and the level of detail provided in your instructions. The big question then becomes, "How do I learn what I need to know about my primary users?"

HOW DO YOU LEARN ABOUT YOUR USERS?

Here are several strategies to help you learn about the users targeted by your technical document:

- Take an inventory of what you do know about your target user group
- Create a profile of the characteristics that distinguish your target user from other types of users
- Interview individuals who fit into your user profile
- Observe individuals who fit your profile using similar types of documents
- Analyze earlier versions of the document to assess how the user had been characterized and note changes, notable strategic choices made by earlier technical communicators, and mismatches with your user profile

Of these strategies, some are more accurate and valuable than others: interviewing members of your target user group is most valuable because you can ask questions; receive valid feedback; and test assumptions about user preferences, approaches, and understanding. Taking an inventory of what you already know about your users can be reliable or not, depending upon your previous experience and knowledge. If you have already conducted interviews and observations of representative members of your user group for an earlier version or similar document, your inventory will likely be most reliable.

To build an inventory of the characteristics that you know about your primary audience, consider these factors:

- Level of experience with the subject matter
- Educational background, both generally and specifically, as related to your topic
- Experience with and attitude toward learning new things
- Experience with and attitude toward technology generally and your topic specifically
- Relevant demographic characteristics such as age, sex, race, socio-economic background or class, culture, and first language

If you do not have information about many of the points above, you will need to do some research to find out where your primary users fall in the spectrum of these different factors.

Interview Users

You can interview representative users to find out about attitudes and levels of expertise. Simultaneously, you can gather information about their preferences for the design and arrangement of instructional information, details that will be useful when you reach the design stage of the project.

Observe Users

Another way to learn about how users use technical documents is to observe them as they use a similar product. This activity resembles a usability test, but it aims to collect general information about the patterns of use of instructional (or other) types of documents.

Interview Experts

If you cannot gain access to representative users, an alternate strategy is to talk to co-workers, fellow technical writers, or knowledgeable peers who will share information with you. When interviewing them, you can test your assumptions about your users against their knowledge and experience. While this option isn't as reliable as talking to actual primary users, it is more effective than guessing.

Create User Profiles

Once you have gathered an inventory of information, use it to create user profiles. User profiles are concise sketches of specific individuals who share characteristics of your primary or target user group. Spend five or ten minutes generating a series of profiles of specific (invented) people who represent various viewpoints from your primary users. See Figure 1.4 for two profiles of potential users for the guide to creating style sheets discussed above.

Develop these profiles to help you think specifically about your users: to consider their attitudes and see them as real people who interact with the text that you will develop. When deciding on specific design or organizational choices for your project, you can make better decisions if you have a concrete idea of who will use this document.

> **IN-CLASS EXERCISE 1.5**
>
> ## Write a User Profile
>
> Write a user profile of yourself as a reader of this chapter. Include whatever demographics you think are relevant, as well as personal characteristics that affect your reading and reception of the information in this chapter.

> **SAMPLE PROFILES**
>
> **Gina**: 50-year-old administrative assistant, BA in history in 1992; self-taught software programs including Word®, PowerPoint®, and Excel®; makes minor changes to department's web pages on Internet to update announcements, etc.; basic user of Dreamweaver but eager to learn more. Ambitious and not afraid of technology.
>
> **Karl**: 27-year-old financial analyst, MBA in 2019; proficient user of various web-based software; owns a small consulting firm supported by website; paid consultant to develop website for him two years ago, but now needs to update it; wants to do this himself. Novice user of Dreamweaver. Concerned about whether he can make the changes that he needs to by himself.

FIGURE 1.4
Sample user profiles.

REACHING YOUR PRIMARY USERS

One way to identify useful strategies for reaching primary users is to look at what other writers have done. Through the choices they make in designing and organizing their information, they illustrate the assumptions they have made about the needs and interests of their users. Lab assignment 1.1 will give you a chance to look at the ways in which several web designers have adapted their information to what they perceive as the needs of their target users. As you explore the different websites, think about which strategies might be useful in your writing.

LAB ASSIGNMENT 1.1

CHARACTERIZING YOUR USERS (AND YOURSELF)

Choose your own favorite website (or find statistics for your Twitter or other social media pages) plus one of the websites listed below, and explore these sites. Using the questions that follow, try to figure out what assumptions the content developers are making about their users' needs. See if you can develop a profile of the type of user that each of the websites addresses through its content and presentation.

a. http://www.tms.org/
b. http://www.useit.com
c. http://www.guinness.com
d. https://pbskids.org/
e. http://www.royal.gov.uk

Generating Ideas for Your Profile

- Who do you think is visiting this website?
- What special characteristics do they have?
- What is their background in the subject matter?
- What attitude toward or level of interest do the site designers assume the user has in the subject?
- Why do you think users will come to this website?
- What tasks might users perform based on the information in this website?
- What legal issues did the website designers have to address regarding this subject matter?
- Is the content of the website directed at a cross-cultural audience? How can you tell?
- What level of technical knowledge does the website assume in the reader/user? How can you tell?

Creating a User Profile for Each Website

Write a paragraph or two about each website in which you create a description of the target users implied in the answers to these questions. Try to include as many different topics as you can to help yourself think about ways in which the users may be different or similar.

Strategies for Reaching Target Users

Now compare the general descriptions using these questions to get started:

- Based on your analysis of these websites, what are four or five ways that users may differ from one another?
- How do these differences affect the kind of information that is included in the writing prepared for them?
- How do these differences affect the visual presentation of the information?

Gathering Analytic Data for Your Websites

If you have Facebook®, LinkedIn®, Twitter, or other social media pages (or your own website), identify what data those companies provide to you as a user. For instance, they usually provide some data about how many connections you have to other users and about your activity on the site.

- Based on what these sites show you, develop a profile of yourself that spans your social media presence.
- What information do you not know but would like to know about who reviews your social media presence?
- Develop strategies to curate or select how you want to be seen on social media: do you want to be seen as a "professional"? family person? fun-loving and idiosyncratic individual?

PURPOSE: WHY ARE YOU WRITING?

Another essential component of the writing situation, besides audience, is purpose or aim: what do you hope to achieve through creating your document? You may have one main purpose or several important goals that you want your user to understand after reading your document. For example, in a memo to co-workers, you might want them to learn that they have one month to review their benefits selections and make any changes they want. The goal of your memo will be fourfold:

1. to get them to read your memo and understand it,
2. to persuade them to review the attached booklet (or visit the informational web page) that outlines their possible choices,
3. to motivate them to act further by making any changes they want, and
4. to do all this before the deadline (e.g., March 31).

You may notice in the previous goals that persuasion and motivation figure centrally in the purpose for writing the memo. If your readers are uninterested in the subject of your memo or they consider themselves too busy to bother with this activity right now (as they meet an important project deadline), they may ignore your message without even skimming it. One of the main rhetorical challenges of this assignment may be to grab readers' attention; another challenge may be to get them to think about their benefits and to make changes to their current selections.

Perhaps you are preparing a report for a client after inspecting the home upon which they have made an offer, conditional on your certifying that it has no major structural flaws. Because the inspection took several hours and you are charging the client $400 for the activity, you want the report to be significant enough to reflect both the cost of the inspection and the care with which you conducted it. Therefore, one of your purposes is to demonstrate that you did inspect the property carefully. A second purpose is to show that you have identified any possible problems with the property. A third purpose is to inform the potential homeowner of where the problems lie so that he or she can decide to either remove the condition or withdraw the offer. Finally, you want your client to be satisfied that the cost of your inspection was a worthwhile expenditure.

Clearly, the writer's reasons for composing a particular document are often complex and multiple. One goal that often characterizes technical documentation is education, its primary purpose being to instruct the reader or user. After all, that is why many of us consult instructions or user manuals—to figure out how to operate a new device or use a software program. And, although instruction may be the primary goal of many technical documents, most texts will also have secondary goals: to inform, to satisfy, to please, to persuade, and so on. The documents that support technological developments also foster good or ill feeling in the target user groups. Technical documents that instruct users quickly and painlessly in how to accomplish the tasks available using the associated product can only foster goodwill, increasing users' desires to try the company's other products based on the positive experience with this one.

HEARING BACK FROM YOUR USERS: RATINGS AND REVIEWS

Technical communication in the social media age benefits from the feedback on documents, videos, and other technical communication products we create. The reviews of the *Strategic Guide to Technical Communication* on Amazon.com, for instance, were helpful to us as we created this book. As instructors, we get reviews of our teaching through student course evaluation feedback at the end of the course. Some students also provide feedback on other social media sites such as Rate My Professor. Twitter provides feedback through comments on a tweet, retweets, likes, and direct messages. LinkedIn provides feedback through likes, comments, and shares. Facebook provides an "Activity Log" that includes likes, comments, and many other indicators of your level of engagement with the platform such as "Others' post to your timeline." Our website (wecanwrite. ca) tells us how many unique visitors came to the site, how many pages they visited, how these numbers have changed over time, and more. The podcast site (https://rogergraves.podomatic.com/) provides details on how many times each episode of the podcast has been listened to, what country listeners come from, how many plays came on mobile devices, and how that podcast compares with other podcasts on higher education topics.

As a consumer, you may have used various sites that provide reviews of products and services, from restaurants and travel-related services to just about any service you can imagine. These sites provide a forum or place for users to give feedback. For technical support documents, comments and feedback about how to perform a task can be posted on discussion forums such as Reddit. As a technical communicator, you want to enable and encourage reviews and feedback from users. You might even consider moderating a user forum so that users can provide feedback and help to each other and so that someone from your organization can respond to requests for help.

WHAT IS GENRE?

The word "genre" was originally a descriptive term classifying documents into neutral groups such as resume, technical report, or user manual. Over the past twenty years, scholarship in the area has led to a more accurate and perceptive definition. In *Genre and the Invention of the Writer*, Anis Bawarshi defines genre as "typified rhetorical strategies communicants use to recognize, organize, and act in all kinds of situations."[4] This definition underscores the characteristics of genre: the structural and rhetorical conventions (i.e., "typified ... strategies"), the organization and presentation of content, and the goals and function of the genre. Genres are used to accomplish actions, and, by selecting one genre over

4   Anis Bawarshi, *Genre and the Invention of the Writer* (Logan: Utah State University Press, 2003), 17.

LAB ASSIGNMENT 1.2

LINKING PURPOSE AND AUDIENCE

Select a document that you've written recently (for example, a job application letter, a report, an essay, a letter, an email message), and reflect on the audience and purpose for this document. Then write several paragraphs answering the following questions:

- Who was your primary reader?
- Did you consider other possible readers? Who were they?
- What did you know about the primary and other readers when you began writing?
- Were you aware of one primary purpose or goal that you were trying to reach with this writing?
- What other goals do you see that you also had in drafting this document?
- What rhetorical or writing strategies did you use to achieve your goals for writing?
- Can you think of other strategies that you might have used to be even more successful in reaching your goals?

another, writers convey specific information that immediately helps readers to understand the purpose of the document. As a student, you are already familiar with the genres of academic writing: summaries, essays, examinations, and other types of papers that rehearse what you've learned and display your understanding of course subject matter and concepts. In academic settings, the specific characteristics of these genres can vary. For example, many instructors distribute an assignment that lists the specific criteria they expect for an essay assignment (use headings, a particular typeface and font size, cite no more than four secondary sources, etc.), and, as you move from discipline to discipline, minor aspects may vary regarding what constitutes an essay. Some minor variations also exist in workplace genres as you move from one organization to another.

STRUCTURAL CONVENTIONS

Each genre has a different structure that reflects what writers are trying to accomplish in using that particular genre. For example, the text in Figure 1.4 is immediately recognizable (even for readers who do not cook) as a standard genre used to instruct people in preparing food: a recipe or instructions for cooking a dish. The list of ingredients, the headings, the numbered steps—these visual elements of the structure of the text signal to readers that this process pertains to food preparation. When readers see the structural elements of a particular genre, they anticipate the specific content associated with that genre structure before they begin reading. If the content does not match reader expectations based on the genre structure (the visual organization of the text), readers will be at least confused (and perhaps annoyed) by the writer's text. For example, Figure 1.5 uses the structure of the recipe genre, but it is not a recipe. Users who need a stew recipe may find Figure 1.5 amusing as a joke, but they may also be irritated at the confusion.

MARINATED PORTOBELLO MUSHROOMS

Marinade

1 tbsp chopped fresh basil
1 tsp chopped fresh garlic
2 tsp balsamic vinegar
2 tbsp olive oil
Sprinkle of freshly ground pepper and salt

Other Ingredients

Six portobello mushrooms
Feta cheese (enough to put some on each mushroom)

To Marinate Mushrooms:

1. Mix marinade at least two hours ahead.
2. Pour half of marinade into a large, flat dish (or a plastic bag).
3. Place mushrooms smooth side down on top of marinade.
4. Drizzle rest of marinade on top of mushrooms.
5. Refrigerate until needed.

To Cook Mushrooms

1. On a preheated barbecue (or on a broiler), grill mushrooms for about 3 minutes on each side.
2. Baste with marinade.
3. Turn stem side up.
4. Fill each cap with feta cheese to taste.
5. Cook for another 3 minutes.
6. Serve hot.

FIGURE 1.4
Example of the genre of recipe instructions.

ELEPHANT STEW

Ingredients

1 elephant
brown gravy
salt and pepper
2 rabbits (optional)

Directions

1. Cut elephant into bite-sized pieces. This should take about two months.
2. Cover with brown gravy.
3. Cook over kerosene fire about 4 weeks at 465 degrees F.

This will serve 3,800 people. If more are expected, 2 rabbits may be added, but do this *only if necessary*, as most people do not like to find a hare in their stew.

FIGURE 1.5
This text subverts the structural conventions of the recipe genre.

RHETORICAL CONVENTIONS

Each genre also has rhetorical conventions—that is, expected purposes or aims that the type of document will accomplish. A writer would never choose to present a business activity update in the form of a technical manual. Nor would a reader consult a manual to gain an activity update. Such a document would confuse the reader expecting to find instructions on how to convert a word-processing file to rich text format. Nor would a manager expect to find a set of instructions on creating rich text format in a subordinate's activity report on her monthly accomplishments. Rhetorically, activity reports document (or inform) and make the argument (or persuade) that the writer worked successfully on assigned tasks over a given time. Readers come to a progress report expecting to be updated on an employee's activities. Again, note that readers have expectations about the rhetorical purpose of a genre as well as about its structure. If a document does not meet its anticipated rhetorical conventions, it is a poor specimen of that genre. The text will not accomplish the action that it was intended to do.

ORGANIZATION AND PRESENTATION OF CONTENT

Not only do genres have structural and rhetorical conventions, they also have rules about how to organize and present the content they contain. Again, this point is about meeting reader and industry expectations, about presenting the content that readers expect in the order that they expect it for a given genre. For example, a technical report does not begin with the appendices or methods used to collect information but with a summary of the key information contained in the main body, as well as any conclusions and recommendations. The report proper begins with an introduction to the topic, outlines the project, describes the scope of the treatment of the topic, identifies how information was collected in researching the topic, and so on, ending with conclusions to the report and recommendations for supervisor action. The organization of material presented in the report follows an established and traditional order that writers use to aid readers in understanding the report's conclusions. When information appears where readers expect it, they can focus attention on the subject and think about the report's argument. As a writer in the workplace, you also make your own job easier if you follow the generic conventions for a document type. Because the organization and presentation are well established for these genres, you can focus your attention on the topic and your treatment of the ideas rather than on how best to convey the basic information to readers. Use a genre's conventions to present information where and how readers expect it.

GOALS AND FUNCTION OF THE GENRE

Each genre has a specific goal (or series of goals) and a function. In the workplace, genres generally aim to facilitate an activity or the promotion of a product. In contrast, academic genres generally have as their goal the demonstration of accomplishment: they demonstrate learning of a subject matter and knowledge competence. For example, essays (a genre staple of academic writing) demonstrate the writer's ability to construct a clear, well-supported argument about an idea or concept. Instructors use them to assess what students have learned and how well an individual might be assembling a conceptual framework for the course material over the school term. From a student's perspective, the goal of this academic genre is to demonstrate an insightful and carefully researched discussion on a particular topic in the course's subject matter. A similar goal—demonstrating knowledge and competence—is also present in the academic genre of examinations and tests. In contrast, workplace genres do not have as a central goal the demonstration of writer competence. Rather, workplace genres aim to achieve action, either by consumers or employees. For example, the white paper or information report (a business genre vaguely resembling that of the academic essay) is a sales tool meant to inform potential consumers about the features and merits of a new product or service. The goal of a white paper is to describe clearly a new product to inform readers and convince them to own this product. Similarly, a genre such as the job application letter functions as a source of information and argument: writers detail their qualifications for a particular job opening and show readers how they are superior to other applicants for this position. The goal of a job application letter is to win an interview for the writer.

GENRE AND ACTIVITY SETS

One way to understand the role that genre plays in workplace, academic, and other types of writing is to consider the activities of an organization (or institution) centered around writing. For example, in education, the goal of learning is focused on taking courses, reading books and articles, listening to lectures, working on problems, and participating in discussions about the information you've learned through reading, listening, and thinking. Many of these activities culminate in the act of writing, either notes to yourself, formal assignments such as papers or exams, problem solutions, or a lab report or set of observations. Some of the writing associated with learning is evaluated, but some of it is self-motivated as a means of learning and understanding aspects and concepts central to the course material. As an experienced student, you are well versed in the activities associated with learning at educational institutions.

Workplaces resemble educational institutions in that they are also activity based, and many of the activities of business, either of a technical communicator, manager, engineer, or lab technician, take place through writing. When you arrive at a co-op or internship placement at a workplace organization, it may not be immediately clear how you can fit into the ongoing activities of your workplace or how you can contribute to these activities. One way to do this may be to participate in drafting all or part of the workplace documents that are generated as part of the organization's productivity. For example, engineers may develop a solution to a manufacturing problem, but, until they draft the report documenting the solution, it is not available to others in the organization. To contribute to the documents that ground an organization's activities, you need to understand the main genre categories that represent the work being done. Rarely do co-workers have the time or opportunity to explain to newcomers the distinguishing generic features of the various documents that ground the organization.

A better way to educate yourself is to explore the document genres archived in your organization. These examples can illustrate the range and characteristics of the types of documents produced in the past by members of your organization. You can study these examples to note features of the different genres to help you understand how the organization defines this genre in this situation. While these types of examples can be useful for indicating general features, be wary of using them as stylistic models for your own versions of such documents. These archived texts are not necessarily good examples of their type, so imitating them can put you in the position of replicating a poor marketing plan or a badly written progress report. Read them and analyze their features critically so that you can begin to separate the mandatory generic features from the poorly written content and organization (in some instances). If you are puzzled about whether a recurring feature is important or just replicated from earlier examples, you can ask your supervisor for input on a specific point. Co-workers are generally happy to help out with targeted questions that can be answered quickly whereas they don't have time to give you a twenty-minute overview on the strengths and weaknesses of a particular sample document. The following sections provide more information on how to analyze the characteristics of a genre that is new to you.

WHAT ARE THE MAIN GENRES OF TECHNICAL COMMUNICATION?

Technical writers expect to produce at least some of the following genres:

- Procedures or instructions
- Manuals
- Reports on technical subject matter
- Specifications
- Proposals
- Letters
- Memos
- Oral presentations

Of this list, the last four genres are broader than just technical communication: they are the primary genres of business and professional writing, and they are related to many of the main activities of business.

WHY DOES GENRE MATTER?

To be considered an educated and experienced professional in your field, you need to know about and be able to produce the principle genres of your field. If you understand the conventions of the genres that you need to write and you have mastered the ability to meet those conventions effectively, then you will be considered a "good" (and maybe even the best) writer of technical communication.

Once you understand and can use the conventions of a genre, you can focus on the writing itself, making the content and presentation as effective as possible. Understanding the basic generic conventions of how to structure instructions helps you to focus on the process of creating the text. Some important purposes of this text are to introduce you to the requirements of the basic genres of technical communication, to provide opportunities for you to practice these genres, and to enable you to build up a portfolio of samples of your best work, which will help you demonstrate your skills and abilities in this area so that you can develop your career options in the area of writing professionally.

HOW DOES ONE ANALYZE A NEW GENRE?

When you examine an unfamiliar genre for the first time, focus on these three aspects to identify its key features:

1. Style
2. Structure
3. Register

Style includes elements such as sentence length, kind, and complexity; word choice; and any use of figurative language such as metaphors. Structure refers to how information or content in a document or genre is organized: is it subdivided into sections? How long is each section? What type of content appears in each section? Register refers to the level of language used in the genre. Is it casual, informal, or formal? Does it use contractions (an indication of informality)? Does it use "I"? The goal of this analysis is to determine what work each paragraph is doing, starting with the introduction, and then assess the paragraphs to decide what each one contributes to the overall purpose of the document.

Analyzing Style

To study the prose style of a genre, collect several examples to ensure that you reach accurate conclusions about it. A stylistic analysis focuses on several features. Count the different elements in the document and calculate the average sentence length, paragraph length, and sentence type. Once you have finished

---

SENTENCE VARIETY
- Simple sentences contain a subject + a verb (e.g., The solution defies belief).
- Compound sentences are two simple sentences joined by a coordinating conjunction (e.g., The solution defies belief, yet it is simple).
- Complex sentences contain a simple sentence (subject + verb) + at least one dependent clause, which also contains a subject and verb (e.g., When you think about it, the solution is simple).
- Compound-complex sentences contain a subject + verb + a dependent clause, as well as an additional simple sentence joined by a coordinating conjunction (e.g., When you think about it, the solution is simple, yet it defies belief).

counting the stylistic features and calculating percentages, examine the numbers to derive some generalizations about how these features are used in the samples. What patterns do you see emerging from the similarities? Use these patterns to imitate the style in your version of the genre.

Analyzing Structure

The second step to analyzing a genre to reproduce it is to examine its structure to determine how the information is organized and presented. One place to start is with what Charles Kostelnick calls the "supratextual" elements, meaning such things as the size of the document, its orientation (portrait or landscape), the type of cover (if any), the binding, and the paper or media of presentation. After assessing the outward qualities of the document, you next explore how the information is organized and presented in the main part of the genre sample. You are looking for such organizational markers as topic sentences, levels of headings, whether it contains chapters, the nature and location of summary information (e.g., an abstract, summary paragraphs at the end of major sections), and so on. Determine what kinds of introductory information are included in the document.

TOPIC SENTENCES

- Assess the use of topic sentences in this genre.

Does every paragraph have a topic sentence?

TRANSITIONAL ELEMENTS

- Locate the transitional phrases or elements that are used to move from one topic to the next.

What is the most common method used to change topics?

METHODS OF IDEA DEVELOPMENT

- Examine the patterns of organization used in the paragraphs.

Based on your analysis, which is the most popular method?

SUMMARY ELEMENTS

- Examine concluding sentences and paragraphs.

What methods are used to conclude a point or discussion?

ANALYZING REGISTER

The final step in analyzing a genre is to determine the register or "form of language customarily used in particular circumstances" (*Concise Oxford Dictionary*). To make this analysis, you should examine the diction of your samples, paying special attention to the tone, level of language, and use of jargon or specialized language, because these are the main sources of information about register. If your analysis shows no use of contractions in your samples (no use of words such as "don't" or "we've"), it suggests that the register or customary level of language for this document is at the "formal" end of the scale.

JARGON, CONVERSATION, ERUDITION

- Count the number of words that are technical or jargon words.
- Count the number of words that are conversational or ordinary.
- Count the number of words that are academic or specialized.
- Calculate the percentage of these types of words against the total number.

What level of language is used in this document? (Is it highly technical? Is it conversational?)

TECHNICAL JARGON (JARGON AND ETHOS)

- Examine how the technical language and jargon is used in the document or genre.

When is jargon used in this type of document (e.g., to establish ethos or credibility of the subject matter; to address other specialists)?

TONE (VOICE/ETHOS OF KNOWLEDGEABLE FRIEND)— CONTRACTIONS AND DICTION

- Count the number of contractions used in the document.

What other techniques (other than using contractions) did the writer use to establish and maintain the level of formality?

Generate a list of the key features and conclusions that your analysis has produced that will be most useful for you as you begin to write your own version of this type of genre.

LAB ASSIGNMENT 1.3

ANALYZING A NEW GENRE

Select two sample documents from a genre that you have never written before. Apply the process of analysis outlined in this chapter to four or five paragraphs from the two samples. When you have completed analyzing the prose style, write a blog post reporting what your major conclusions are about the principal features of this genre. Address the post to your classmates to help them understand quickly the distinguishing characteristics of the genre that you analyzed. Submit your post to the electronic class site for your course as part of a discussion thread.

WHAT ARE GENRE SETS?

"Genre sets" are groups of documents that go together. Documents can "go together" in different ways. Genre sets can include documents that contain the same information but use different genres to address their audience and achieve their purpose. For example, Figures 1.6 and 1.7 form this type of set. Fig. 1.6 is a Quick Guide, a two-page document that briefly summarizes research on a topic, highlights conclusions, and offers three or four specific suggestions for action, and a few central sources for readers who want more information about the topic. The Quick Guide in Fig. 1.6 targets post-secondary instructors of academic writing and aims to coach them on how to respond to grammatical errors in their students' school assignments. Fig. 1.7 is a short article that informs readers about the content of a podcast on the same topic for the same audience but with a different purpose. Instead it aims to invite readers to listen to the podcast for more detailed information. Genre sets can also initiate specific sequences of documents. For example, if a software development firm publishes a request for proposals (**RFP**) to document a new program developed by their engineers, you, as an independent technical communicator, may respond with a proposal outlining your plan to create the manuals for the project. The RFP, the proposals that are written in response, and the documents that are created as a solution to the problem outlined in the RFP all make up a "genre set." In these genre sets, one initial document sets in motion the need for other documents to be written in response. The interrelation of these documents constitutes some of the important activities of a business organization.

Grammar and Errors in Student Writing

Roger Graves

What Does Writing Studies Research Say?

Bean (2011) offers an excellent summary of the research in writing studies regarding grammar. Perhaps the best place to start, however, is with Hartwell's definitions of grammar: Grammar 1 = native speaker's innate knowledge of their native tongue; Grammar 2 = linguistic sciences' descriptions of the way language works; Grammar 3 = linguistic etiquette/usage; Grammar 4 = school grammar; Grammar 5 = stylistic grammar.

Grammar 1 is known to all school-aged children and adults. Grammar 2 is a scientific model of Grammar 1, and it is not useful in learning Grammar 1 for native speakers of English. Grammar 3 is not grammar at all but usage. Grammar 4 is, in Hartwell's terms, "unconnected with anything remotely resembling literate adult behavior" (p. 364). Grammar 5, or style, can be taught either implicitly through extensive use of the language (one school of thought) or explicitly through the study of prose style (the other school of thought).

Clearly we cannot teach Grammar 1 or (unless we are teaching a linguistics course) Grammar 2. Grammar 3, or usage, and Grammar 5, style, is similarly outside of the usual focus for instructors in courses that are not focused on writing. Grammar 4, school grammar, has been the subject of hundreds of studies since 1900.

Pressure to teach grammar as a way to eliminate errors in student writing comes from assumptions about these grammars. As Connors and Lunsford (1988) showed, however, the rate of errors in student writing per 100 words has remained relatively constant over the last century at about two (345). In a survey of research into the various ways grammar has been taught over this period, Smith, Cheville, and Hillocks (2008) found that hundreds of studies of various methods of teaching traditional school grammar to improve the quality of student writing are at best ineffective. At worst, they take time away from strategies that do work to improve student writing (process approaches, genre approaches), and they also focus assessment on surface errors and correctness—two features of writing that are easier to identify and appear "objective." School systems create tests that focus on errors and correctness at the expense of audience and purpose, and the result is that students may be able to produce "clean" texts that communicate very little.

Where Do Errors Come From?

Research with student writers at the university level shows that they are capable of correcting the majority of errors they make. Many errors result from poor editing/proofreading proofreading (Haswell 1983, quoted in Bean p. 75), and Bartholomae showed how students self-correct when reading texts aloud (1980, quoted in Bean p. 75).

Mina Shaughnessy, working with open enrollment students at the City University of New York, showed how errors are best seen as failed attempts by student writers to grow and develop. Without these errors, those students would not try new prose structures and therefore not improve. She advocated that instructors look for patterns of errors in student writing, bring those patterns to the attention of the students, and then work to correct the underlying mistaken rule that students were applying.

Implications for Instructors

Bean points out that the number of student errors increases with the cognitive difficulty of the assignment (77). If instructors ask students to write in an unfamiliar genre, or ask them to create a large (20 page plus) assignment, they can expect the number of student errors to increase. Instructors can exacerbate the problem through their grading practices: while the best students benefit from having errors pointed out on their marked papers, for the rest of the class this practice demoralizes them and does the work of finding errors for them (Bean 78–9).

1. Structure your assignment deadlines and evaluation schemes to require students to proofread and edit their work.
2. Communicate to your students the specific kinds of errors that you find unacceptable.
3. Ignore or minimize the importance of "accent" errors in non-native speakers' written texts.
4. Focus your efforts on identifying patterns of errors in student writing, and work with students on correcting the incorrect rule they apply that generates the surface error.

Further Reading

Bean, J. (2011). *Engaging ideas: The professor's guide to integrating writing, critical thinking, and active learning in the classroom*. (2nd Ed.). San Francisco: Jossey-Bass.

Hartwell, P. (1985). "Grammar, Grammars, and the Teaching of Grammar." *College English* 47: 105–27. Rpt. In Cheryl Glenn, Melissa Goldthwaite, & Robert Connors. (2003). *The St. Martin's guide to teaching writing*. (5th Ed.). Boston: Bedford/St. Martin's.

Hillocks, G. (1986). *Research on written composition*. Urbana, IL: ERIC Clearing House on Reading and Communication Skills.

Smith, M., Cheville, J., and Hillocks, G. (2008). "'I guess I'd better watch my English': Grammars and the Teaching of English Language Arts." In MacArthur, C., Graham, S., and Fitzgerald, J. (2008). *Handbook of writing research*. New York: Guilford.

Walvoord, B. and Johnson-Anderson, V. (2010). *Effective grading: A tool for learning and assessment*. (2nd Ed.). San Francisco: Jossey-Bass.

FIGURE 1.6
A Quick Guide summarizes research on a topic, conclusions, and recommends specific actions.
Source: https://cloudfront.ualberta.ca/-/media/centre-for-teaching-and-learning/wac/quick-guides/wacgrammarand errorsinstudentwriting.pdf.

Grammar: Grade it or not?

Published on September 11, 2018   ✐ **Edit article** | ⬈ **View stats**

For instructors who are not teaching a writing course, how much attention should they give to grammar errors and proficiency in student writing? In a business context, the issue presents itself differently, and I'll talk about that in a future podcast. For instructors at post-secondary institutions, though, this presents something of problem.

Students sometimes resent losing grades for grammar and punctuation errors because "this isn't an English course!" But for instructors who are aware that writing proficiency is part of the graduation outcomes for university degrees, not pointing out errors in grammar and punctuation can seem like they are not helping students achieve that important outcome. So what should they do?

In this podcast I review the research that explores how effective it is to teach grammar to native speakers of English at post-secondary schools. I then review the social issues around enforcing Standard Edited English before offering some positions instructors can take when they prepare rubrics or scoring guides to help them grade student work.

Figure 1.7
This short article invites readers to listen to a short discussion on teaching grammar as part of writing instruction.

EVALUATING SOCIAL MEDIA PROFILES (AKA PREPARING FOR THE JOB SEARCH)

An interesting example of a genre set is the overall impression created by an individual's social media platform. Each platform addresses a different kind of audience and creates a version of the account holder. When the versions are combined, you obtain an overall impression of that individual. If you conduct an Internet search of that individual, the locations and media where they have been tagged by friends and family members creates yet another dimension of the profile. What is the cumulative impression of all of these dimensions?

Part 1. For the first part of this project, choose a public figure who has a social media presence online. You can choose an athlete, a politician, a celebrity, an actor, a member of a royal family, etc. Investigate three or four of the platforms that this individual uses to create his or her presence. Analyze the material that is posted, and take notes of what you observe. Your goal is to compile a description of this public figure as represented in the materials that you analyze from the platforms that you visit. You may also include some information from other sites where that individual is tagged, if you want to also consider how he/she is represented through other people's postings.

1. Based on your research, prepare 5–10 slides on the social media profile of your selected public figure in which you present your findings (with evidence) and conclusions about him or her. Your audience for these slides is your classmates and instructor.
2. Post your slide deck on your class learning management system (LMS).
3. Review your classmates' postings and, as your instructor directs, either

   i) prepare several comments or follow-up questions about your classmates' findings to contribute to a class discussion, or
   ii) prepare a three-minute presentation to give in class based on your slides that summarizes your research and findings.

Part 2. Another example of a genre set is job application materials (that is, the position advertised, qualification application database, letter of application, resume, etc.). While a cover letter, resume, and references used to be employers' sole sources of information that allowed candidates to curate potential employers' impressions of them before an interview, social media now adds many complex layers of information. Employers now search numerous social media platforms to supplement any application materials to determine whether a candidate may be an appropriate "fit" for their organization.

In Part 2 of this project, aim to answer these questions:

■ What does the social media profile say about the account holder as a potential job candidate?
■ How should the account holder change this social media profile to improve his or her self-presentation as a desirable potential employee?

You have two choices for selecting a social media profile to analyze:

   i) you can analyze your own,
   ii) you can choose a partner in the class and analyze your partner's profile.

Your goal for this project is to analyze and evaluate a social media profile as a whole and to make recommendations about what changes should be made to each site to optimize the impression created through the materials posted there.

MAJOR PROJECT 1.1 (CONT.)

Here are some steps to follow:

1. List all of the apps used by the account holder and decide whether to look at all of them or choose only three or four.
2. Note the privacy settings for each account.
3. Investigate each account in detail, making sure you look at all the photographs, all the links or articles posted, comments, etc.
4. Take notes about specific details regarding all of the material that you look at.
5. Analyze the posted materials to assess what they tell you about the individual(s) depicted in each account.
6. Assess the conclusions that can be made about the account holder based on your analysis of the site content.
7. Evaluate the overall impression you have of the account holder based on all the sites and their postings.
8. Recommend three to five specific changes the account holder should make to the sites to ensure they represent themselves as a suitable/appropriate/outstanding potential employee.

When you complete your research and analysis and compile your findings, write a memo report addressed to your instructor (and your partner, if you are analyzing his/her profile) in which you present your findings and make specific recommendations as to how to improve/optimize how the account holder is characterized in the social media profile. Your report should include the following:

1. Describe the problem you addressed.
2. Describe how you solved the problem (describe which sites you visited, how you analyzed the information in each site, and how you drew conclusions based on your analysis).
3. Explain your conclusions.
4. Recommend three to five specific actions your client should take to optimize his/her characterization as a desirable potential employee.

CHAPTER TWO

Ethical Issues of Technical Communication

If you had free reign over classified networks for long periods of time ... say, 8–9 months ... and you saw incredible things, awful things ... things that belonged in the public domain, and not on some server stored in a dark room in Washington DC ... What would you do?

—Chelsea Manning[1]

Ethics may have been the last thing you thought you would encounter in a textbook on technical communication. After all, what have values got to do with writing procedures? The answer depends on what the procedures are for. Steven Katz[2] has reported on Nazi recommendation reports that explain how to improve the death vans used to exterminate Jews. As an employee, you might think encountering that kind of text, or agreeing to work on it, unlikely. However, at some point in your career, you may be asked or pressured to write something that is either less than wholly truthful or downright false. Or you may be asked to write about new ways to slaughter farm animals; if you are a vegetarian, that might present a problem for you since it asks you to help others to engage in behaviors that result in actions you disapprove of.

The link between ethics and communication has been debated for over two thousand years, beginning with Aristotle and his comments about the good character (or "ethos") of the person speaking or writing giving rise to trust. Aristotle said that the truth of any situation would always come out eventually and that listeners could judge the character of the speaker from his or her words. Quintilian, a Roman rhetorician, went so far as to say that only a good man (a virtuous, honest man) would be believable. However, recent history suggests instead that ethically challenged individuals can be quite believable. The key here may be that they really believed what they wrote or said at the time they said it.

ETHICS FRAMEWORKS

Ethics is an abstract term. To think through ethical decisions, we sometimes look to "frameworks" or groups of principles that have been developed to guide decision making. In the medical field, for example, Beauchamp and Childress identified four principles for making biomedical decisions:[3]

- Respect for autonomy
- Beneficence (balance benefits and risks for the patient)
- Non-malfeasance (avoid causing harm)
- Justice (treat people fairly)

1 Quoted (under the name Bradley Manning) in Kevin Poulsen and Kim Zetter, "WikiLeaks' 400,000 Iraq War Documents Reveal Torture, Civilian Deaths," *Wired*, October 22, 2010, http://www.wired.com/threatlevel/2010/10/wikileaks-press.

2 Steven Katz, "The Ethic of Expediency: Classical Rhetoric, Technology, and the Holocaust," *College English* 54, no. 3 (1992): 255–75.

3 UK Clinical Ethics Network, "Ethical Frameworks: The Four Principles of Biomedical Ethics," UK Clinical Ethics Network, accessed February 9, 2020, http://www.ukcen.net/ethical_issues/ethical_frameworks/the_four_principles_of_biomedical_ethics. For more information see Tom L. Beauchamp and James F. Childress, *Principles of Biomedical Ethics*, 5th ed. (Oxford: Oxford University Press, 2001).

Outlining an Ethical Position

Use the ethical frameworks outlined above to write a one-page (500-word) position paper on the WikiLeaks release of 400,000 documents related to the Iraq war. To find out more about the release of these documents, search the web for "wikileaks and war logs." The search results will lead you to both primary sources (the documents that have been made public) and secondary sources (news articles describing those documents). In class, examine the release of these documents from as many of the ethical frameworks as you can: take notes, discuss the implications of each framework, and try out thesis statements for positions that you might argue in favor of. In your position paper, examine the release of this information from the perspective of at least two ethical frameworks: utilitarian, rights, justice, common good, and virtue ethics. In your conclusion, identify which of the frameworks—or which combination of frameworks—helps you describe your position on the release of these documents.

The Markkula Center for Applied Ethics at Santa Clara University summarizes five common ethical frameworks that span a wide variety of contexts:[4]

- The utilitarian approach: choose the action that produces the greatest good and the least harm
- The rights approach: choose the action that protects the moral rights (freedom, privacy, choice, information) of those who are affected by the decision
- The fairness or justice approach: treat everyone equally or fairly
- The common good approach: choose the action that contributes most to the common good
- The virtue approach: choose the action that is consistent with virtuous values such as honesty, compassion, tolerance, integrity, and prudence

The American Society of Mechanical Engineers (ASME) maintains an online "Ethics in Engineering" center that contains links to an online discussion forum, the society's "Code of Ethics of Engineers," and several self-study modules in various formats, including one on the web: "Ethics for Engineers: Doing the Right Thing When No One is Looking" (http://www.asme.org/NewsPublicPolicy/Ethics/Ethics_Center.cfm). ASME also provides a link to the W. Maurice Young Centre for Applied Ethics at the University of British Columbia, whose faculty members have developed "A Framework for Ethical Decision-Making: Version 6.0 Ethics Shareware."[5] In that document, McDonald, Rodney, and Starzomski describe one way to proceed with decisions ethically:

1. Collect information and identify the problem.
2. Specify feasible alternatives.
3. Use your ethical resources to identify morally significant factors in each alternative.
4. Propose and test possible resolutions.
5. Make your choice.

Step 3 draws upon the frameworks described previously in this section, the one useful in biomedical contexts and, even more generally, the frameworks based on the utilitarian, rights, justice, common good, and virtue approaches.

ETHICS FOR STUDENTS

Many large organizations create statements that reflect their values and offer guidelines for those who work for the organizations, and sometimes even for

4   Markkula Center for Applied Ethics, "A Framework for Ethical Decision Making," Markkula Center for Applied Ethics, Santa Clara University, accessed February 9, 2020, https://www.scu.edu/ethics/ethics-resources/ethical-decision-making/a-framework-for-ethical-decision-making/.

5   Michael McDonald, Paddy Rodney, and Rose Starzomski, "A Framework for Ethical Decision-Making: Version 6.0 Ethics Shareware," The W. Maurice Young Centre for Applied Ethics, University of British Columbia, accessed April 6, 2011, https://ethics.ubc.ca/files/2014/11/A-Framework-for-Ethical-Decision-Making.pdf.

those who work with them. For example, Western University offers the following student code of conduct:

> The University ... is a community of students, faculty and staff involved in learning, teaching, research, and other activities. The University seeks to provide an environment of free and creative inquiry within which critical thinking, humane values, and practical skills are cultivated and sustained. It is committed to a mission and to principles that will foster excellence and create an environment where its students, faculty, and staff can grow and flourish.... Students are responsible for observing a standard of conduct that will contribute to the University's mission and that will support an environment conducive to the intellectual and personal growth of all who study, work and live here. This responsibility includes respecting the rights, property, and well-being of other members of the University community and visitors to the campus and not engaging in conduct that could reasonably be seen to endanger or adversely affect the health, safety, rights, security or property of the University, its members and visitors. (*Source: http://www.uwo.ca/univsec/pdf/board/code.pdf*)

This statement covers a lot of ground by using general terms such as "free and creative inquiry" and the "proper functioning" of all programs offered by the university. One activity that would be headed off by this statement is the occupation of university offices by student protesters, something that did happen at some universities in the 1960s and 1970s.

While occupying the office of the president of your college or university may not be on your agenda, avoiding plagiarism should be. Most, if not all, colleges and universities have plagiarism policies to enforce academic honesty—ethics. It is important to the "proper functioning" of these institutions that those who study and work at them give credit to others when credit is due, for example, when a professor uses the ideas, research, or words of earlier scholars. All of us depend on the work of others to do our work; we read the books and articles that others have written before we write our own essays and articles. Referencing systems help us locate relevant passages in texts others have written and make clear what are our own contributions to the academic conversation.

At college or university, much of the writing you will be asked to do will focus on you demonstrating what you know about a certain topic. One of the key functions of citation systems is to impress upon your readers that you know about (and have read) the important articles or books in the area you are studying. If you do not cite your sources, you lose the opportunity to impress your readers. More specifically, often there are differing positions within an area of study—conflicting positions, different "camps," differing theoretical approaches to gathering data. You can show that you understand that more than one approach will suffice and that you know what the approaches are through your references to these bodies of work. So references are not just ways to cover yourself from charges of plagiarism; they can also be ways to further impress your instructors with what you know and the depth of your research.

Most discussions of plagiarism assume that students do it but aren't victims of it. As a writer, you should know that you hold copyright to your own work: your essays, reports, and manuals are works you have created. Consequently, you own the copyright to them. And while that may not seem like much in the context of writing a typical essay as a student, the documents you write in a technical communication course may very well hold value for others. Many students in our technical communication classes have written office procedure manuals for their workplaces, brochures, manuals for updating extensive websites they manage, procedures for running cross-generational housing complexes, and so on. These documents have real value to the organizations that the students created them for, and those students should have the rights to reproduce them should they have commercial value. Other students have published essays in magazines; while usually they sign away the copyright to those works, they should be aware of the value that these documents represent. As someone who is working to improve your writing skills, you should think ahead to creating a venue for your writing—perhaps a blog or a website. As the author of either of those kinds of publications, you are the copyright holder. You want others to link to your site, but you also want to prevent others from copying your work and using it on their site as if they had written it. As you become a better writer and seek a wider audience for your work, you become the person whose work is being used by others. Citation systems codify the established ways of using the work of others.

You can find all sorts of style guides that will tell you how to format references according to the Modern Language Association (MLA) rules, the American Psychological Association (APA) rules, The Chicago Manual of Style (CMS) of the University of Chicago Press, and the Council of Science Editors (CSE) style. Here are a few online sources:

FIGURE 2.1
Websites where you can find more information about how to cite sources correctly, according to the documentation style chosen.

APA	**Purdue University** https://owl.purdue.edu/owl/research_and_citation/apa_style/apa_style_introduction.html **Thompson Rivers University** https://tru.ca/_shared/assets/apastyle31967.pdf
CMS	**University of Chicago Press** http://www.chicagomanualofstyle.org/home.html **Simon Fraser University Libraries** https://www.lib.sfu.ca/help/cite-write/citation-style-guides/chicago/author-date
CSE	**Thompson Rivers University** https://www.tru.ca/library/pdf/csecitationstyle.pdf **University of Wisconsin-Madison** https://writing.wisc.edu/handbook/documentation/doccse/nameyear/
MLA	**Concordia University** http://library.concordia.ca/help/howto/mla.php **University of Wisconsin-Madison** https://writing.wisc.edu/handbook/documentation/docmla/

But to use these sources properly, you need to make good notes while you are researching. That is, you need to record:

- page numbers accurately,
- dates that you accessed a web page,
- quotations from the original sources accurately, and
- details of publication.

Without this information, you will be unable to write complete citations, and your readers will be unable to find the sources you send them to.

Providing a complete and properly formatted list of references is good, but even more important is working these references into your argument. If you can incorporate references into your writing through well-written summaries of the research you refer to, your writing will be judged superior. And, if that isn't enough, it will also be a fair or ethical representation of the original article or text. A good summary briefly (in a few sentences) communicates the gist of the original work to your readers. That is, you tell your readers what you think they should or need to know about the material written by someone else. Begin your summary by providing an overview of the original article, a fairly abstract or general statement of what it is about. Then write one or more specific statements that indicate what topic or idea within that general topic you think should be of interest to your reader. When you have explained in enough detail (this could be as little as a clause within a sentence or as much as several sentences or even a paragraph), provide a reference to the original article (the format will differ depending on which documentation system you are using).

In the context of academic writing, citing and referencing are basic building blocks of ethical work. You are immersed in a world of texts when you pursue college or university education, and, to demonstrate that you belong, you need to refer to these texts and show you understand them. Doing this correctly proves your membership and establishes your credibility in the higher education community. For more information about citing and paraphrasing sources, see also Chapter 3, "Researching Technical Subjects."

HOW IS ETHICS RELATED TO TECHNICAL COMMUNICATION?

Technical communication changes the dynamic usually associated with plagiarism of essays and reports at school. While at school you write to demonstrate what you know to an already knowledgeable reader; technical communication fulfills a different function. Instead, much technical communication aims to educate and inform readers about how to operate a piece of equipment or a software application. As a result, the focus is less on demonstrating factual knowledge and more on demonstrating the skilful use of ways of explaining or informing readers. Copying a paragraph from some other source doesn't answer the demands of the rhetorical situation of a good technical communication assignment: the level of knowledge of the reader usually differs from that of whatever source you might find, and so does the scope of what is being explained. In addition, because much technical communication is done badly, plagiarizing deliberately becomes counterproductive.

Working technical writers, then, face ethical challenges that differ from those faced in typical academic contexts. One of these differences has to do with authorship. When a technical writer produces a report or manual for an organization, the organization owns the copyright to that text. The text can then be "reused" in other reports and manuals that the organization produces. This writing, sometimes referred to as "boilerplate" text, can be reused in other documents. Much of the text in standard legal documents, such as wills, fits this description and use. So when you are writing documents that will come out under the corporation's name, the reuse of boilerplate text does not fit under the category of plagiarism. However, technical writers face other ethical challenges.

One area of ethical choice involves how to give credit to others for work that is theirs. Copyright symbols, trademark symbols, and referencing systems (APA, MLA, and CMS) are some of the ways writers give credit to others. As a technical writer, you need to become familiar with the proper use of these symbols and referencing systems as a way to ensure that you do not appear to be taking credit for the work of others.

COPYRIGHT, TRADEMARKS, AND PATENTS

Copyright refers to the right to copy or otherwise reproduce original works yourself and the right to assign to others permission to make copies. This right applies to original works of literature, film, music, and art. Originality can be a hard concept to determine—think of remixes of old songs. Which part is original, and which part is new? Another difficult part of copyright is defining what a "substantial" part of it would be: one rule is that you can photocopy for reference one chapter of a book provided it amounts to less than 20 per cent of the book it was taken from. (Note that the right to "copy" less than 20 per cent of a book does not equal the right to reuse or reprint this text.)

You should label your own work with your (or your organization's) name, the year in which the work was first published, and the copyright symbol: ©. This labeling ensures your work will be protected in other countries that adhere to the Universal Copyright Convention, and where such a requirement is mandatory. Although this label is not obligatory in Canada or the United States after 1989, the copyright symbol serves to remind others that the work is copyright protected. In this era of digital publication, you would be wise to adopt this symbol as part of the standard way you create a document.

"Fair dealing" is the term used under the copyright laws of Canada to describe an exception to the small amount of a work that can be copied without seeking permission. Fair use includes making enlarged copies of print materials for visually challenged students. Non-profit educational institutions can make copies if the copies are used on campus for educational purposes. For a detailed description of many copyright issues, contact the Canadian Intellectual Property Office (http://www.ic.gc.ca/eic/site/cipointernet-internetopic.nsf/eng/home), or, for information concerning copyrighted materials and for licenses to reprint this material, consult the Canadian copyright licensing agency, Access Copyright (http://www.accesscopyright.ca). Note, however, that many works are not available to be reproduced at a post-secondary educational institution in Canada, including

- unpublished works,
- any materials intended for one-time use (such as workbooks),
- commercial newsletters,
- originals of artistic works (including photographs and prints),
- print music, and
- works that are excluded. (Contact Access Copyright for further information or consult your license at your place of employment.)

In the five years between 2005 and 2010, three bills were tabled in the Canadian Parliament to revise the Copyright Act; none were passed.

In the United States, copies can be made at non-profit educational institutions according to the Copyright Office's definition of fair use (http://www.copyright. gov/title17/92chap1.html#107). Despite these guidelines, the concept of fair use remains elastic. One person who used the name of an imaginary planet in a Star Wars™ movie was forced to surrender the web address to Lucasfilm Ltd. or face a civil lawsuit from the company.[6] The website never had any copyrighted works on it; it was just that the name had been created as part of the series of films, and the company asserted that the name alone was something valuable that could be protected. Ironically, the name—Tatooine—was itself derived from a real city in Tunisia called Tataouine. If the creator of the website had used the real city's name, he could not have been sued. But protecting single words seems to be a new limitation on fair use. Trademarks refer to items that establish a brand: slogans, product names, packaging, and symbols. As a technical writer, you would probably encounter this in your references to existing trademarks held by your company or another company's products that work with your company's products; a reference to Microsoft® Word should have the trademark symbol affixed to it. Trademarks differ from patents in that they are not registered.

Patents refer to inventions such as new manufacturing products and processes. Usually, you would encounter them only by referring to them in texts that you write. Recently, some companies have patented human genetic sequences that they alter. DEKALB® is a new type of corn developed by Monsanto, for example, and you should refer to it using the registered trademark symbol.

6 Anne Broache, "Free Speech under Net Attack, Study Says," *CNET News*, December 6, 2005, news. cnet.com/2100-1030_3-5983072. html.

WHAT IS NOT COPYRIGHTABLE

While the actual text of an article, novel, manual, or website is copyrightable, in Canada, some aspects of original works may not be. Figure 2.2 gives examples where copyright does not apply:

Titles for a song, slogans	"Rockin' in the Free World"
The idea for a plot	Woman elected president or prime minister
A work in the public domain	*Hamlet*
The facts in the article	Barrick Gold was up $1.06 to $31.26
The name of the program	Microsoft® Word™
(However, this might be protected through a trademark registration)	

FIGURE 2.2
Examples of items that cannot be copyrighted.
Source: Purdue University Copyright Office, "Copyright Overview," accessed January 31, 2019, https://www.lib.purdue. edu/uco/CopyrightBasics/basics.html.

RULES FOR COPYING IMAGES

Images add much to your work as a technical writer, but you may not have the time to create images or take photographs for the publications you produce. For many people, the web provides a tempting source of images because they can quickly select, right click, and "Save As" to grab an image from someone else's web page. But remember that, unless you have paid a fee to the photographer who took the photograph or the artist who created the image you want to use, you do not have permission to copy that visual.[7] If you lack a budget to pay for artwork, a better way to find appropriate graphics is to search for royalty-free images. A good place to start is www.freedigitalphotos.net, a website from the United Kingdom that provides free downloads of over 6,000 images. If you are using Microsoft® Office products, make use of the extensive collection of images available on your desktop or through links to Microsoft's website.

If your technical communication project has a budget, spend some of it to pay someone to create appropriate visuals or purchase some ready-made illustrations for your documents. As a student, however, it is unlikely that you have a budget for purchasing visuals, but with most cell phones' high-resolution cameras, you can take photographs and insert them into your documents as illustrations. If you are documenting software procedures, you can use your computer's screen capture software to illustrate key steps. All of these techniques are free from copyright restrictions. But remember: if you took photographs to include in a brochure or newsletter for the company you work for, those photographs are owned by the company, not you. Similarly, if you take photographs of people who can be identified, you cannot legally use those photographs in advertisements or for commercial purposes without their permission. For more information about laws regarding street photography (taking photos in public), expertphotography.com has a useful overview by state and country.

7 Canadian Intellectual Property Office, "Photographs," *Copyright Circulars* 11 (July 1, 1998).

WRITING ETHICALLY

Although it may seem obvious that what you write should be accurate and true, in practice, there is considerable leeway between what may be factually correct and how you represent the facts in the documents you create. How many times have you read or heard references to the "spin" various political handlers put on a candidate's or politician's remarks? How often do you read headlines like these?

- "Pressed on the ACA [Affordable Care Act], Trump's Rhetoric Takes an Incoherent Turn" (Steve Bennen, *MSNBC*, March 6, 2020)
- "NDP Trapped by Its Own Rhetoric on Corporate Taxes" (*Calgary Herald*, March 12, 2019, Opinion)
- "Republicans' Extreme Abortion Rhetoric Isn't Just Wrong, It's Dangerous" (*Intelligencer* [New York], February 28, 2019)

Each headline refers to *rhetoric* as a way of framing the topic that is being talked about. In each case, the authors take the position that this framing or way of talking about the issue will not result in progress toward a resolution of the problem under discussion.

As a technical communication student, you will have to make choices about how you want to frame the topics you write about. Although the results are unlikely to be as loaded as the headlines quoted above, you will, nevertheless, decide on at least one main factor: how clear do you want to be in your writing?

Many people take it as a given that all writers should strive for clarity in everything that they write, and, at first glance, this would seem to be self-evident— when would you not want to be clear? It turns out, however, that there are many legitimate situations in which you would not want to be clear: bad news, for example, should usually be delivered after a buffer statement of some kind. It would be cruel to simply walk up to someone and announce that he or she was fired or had failed a test or to tell a person bluntly that a family member had died. On a resume, you may not want to be clear about employment history if there is a gap in your employment record that would make you a less desirable candidate. In addition to these sorts of situations, many organizations often use language to hide the truth of a situation. They write in a deliberately vague way, use euphemisms, and organize information so that key components are buried in a document's fine print. Advertisements for mobile phone companies often refer to the fine print at the bottom of the page. Plain language laws and initiatives came about as a solution to this kind of strategically unclear language use.

Pennsylvania's "Plain Language Consumer Contract Act" explains the need for plain language this way: "The General Assembly finds that many consumer contracts are written, arranged and designed in a way that makes them hard for consumers to understand. Competition would be aided if these contracts were easier to understand ... This act will protect consumers from making contracts that they do not understand. It will help consumers to know better their rights and duties under those contracts."[8]

8 Pennsylvania Plain Language Consumer Contract Act (June 23, 1993), *P.S.* § 2202, http://www.languageandlaw.org/TEXTS/STATS/PLAINENG.HTM.

Plain language definitions vary, but the essence of plain language is directness: write short sentences using specific, uncomplicated terms that your readers can understand quickly. This definition applies as much to government publications, legal writing, and scientific writing as it does to technical communication. Of course, sometimes trying to simplify language can create problems, as in the examples in Figure 2.3.

FIGURE 2.3

Examples of technical phrases and what they really mean.

Source: Plain Language, "Technical Terms in Plain English," accessed March 9, 2020, https://www.plainlanguage. gov/resources/humor/technical-terms-in-plain-english/.

A number of different approaches are being tried.	We are still clueless.
An extensive report is being prepared on a fresh approach to the problem.	We just hired three kids fresh out of college.
Preliminary operational tests were inconclusive.	The darn thing blew up when we threw a switch.

However, there are obvious differences between language that is just putting the best spin on a possibly unpleasant fact, as in the phrases quoted in Figure 2.3, and language that deliberately seeks to confuse readers or discourage them from asking questions. For example, Figure 2.4 presents some examples of phrases that are not direct and clear, together with their translations.

FIGURE 2.4

Before and after plain language.

Source: Plain Language, "Wordiness Made Spare," accessed March 12, 2020, https://www.plainlanguage.gov/ examples/before-and-after/wordiness/.

Before	Revised
Sections 4.40 through 4.71 do not apply to Indian probate proceedings, heirship determinations under the White Earth Reservation Land Settlement Act of 1985, and other proceedings under subpart D of this part, except that §§ 4.40 through 4.71 do apply to cases referred to an administrative law judge pursuant to § 4.337(a)	Unless a case is referred to an administrative law judge under § 4.337(a), §§ 4.40 through 4.71 do not apply to: • Indian probate proceedings; • Heirship determinations under the White Earth Reservation Land Settlement Act of 1985; and • Other proceedings under subpart D of this part.
The Dietary Guidelines for Americans recommends a half hour or more of moderate physical activity on most days, preferably every day. The activity can include brisk walking, calisthenics, home care, gardening, moderate sports exercise, and dancing.	Do at least 30 minutes of exercise, like brisk walking, most days of the week.

PLAIN LANGUAGE GUIDELINES

At its heart, plain language involves an ethical relationship between the reader and writer. As a writer, you must want to communicate with your readers clearly. To do this, you will take their point of view and write what has been called "reader-based prose" or prose that is organized around what the reader needs to know. Rather than writing down everything you know about a topic to show off your knowledge or in the faint hope that readers will be able to sort through your text to find what they are looking for, you will take some time to investigate who is reading your work:

- What level of knowledge do they have?
- What is their cultural background?
- What is their income level?
- What do they want to know?
- What information will they use most frequently?
- What questions are they asking about the topic you are writing about?

Asking and answering these kinds of questions demonstrates your concern and consideration for your readers. The information you generate from this exercise will help you make decisions about how to organize your document and what kinds of vocabulary to use. See Chapter 1, "Audience, Purpose, Genre, and Medium," for more information and specific guidelines for learning more about your readers.

Once you have gathered some data about your readers, you can use that data to decide how to organize your information in ways that respond to their concerns. One popular and effective way to organize information is through a series of questions with answers. If you've researched your readers' needs well, you can organize your document around the questions you know readers will have. And, of course, how you write can significantly affect how easily your readers can understand your writing. For strategies to write clearly and plainly see Chapter 4, "Writing Technical Prose." Finally, to ensure you use visuals ethically, follow standard practices so that your readers can tell if there are gaps in data. Chapter 5, "Visual Technical Communication," goes into more detail on that subject. Figure 2.5 lists additional sources of information about copyright, fair use, and plain language.

Organization	Website Address
Access Copyright	http://www.accesscopyright.ca
Canadian Intellectual Property Office	http://www.cipo.ic.gc.ca/eic/site/cipointernet-internetopic.nsf/eng/h_wr00003.html
United States Copyright Office	http://www.copyright.gov
Copyright and Fair Use, Stanford University Libraries	http://fairuse.stanford.edu
Copyright Society of the U.S.A.	http://www.csusa.org
Plain Language	http://www.plainlanguage.gov
Plain Language Commission (UK)	http://www.clearest.co.uk

FIGURE 2.5
Resources on copyright, fair use, and plain language.

IN-CLASS EXERCISE 2.2

Using Plain Language

1. Examine the text in Figure 2.6, "Class 5: Oxidizing Substances and Organic Peroxides." This passage discusses how to classify types of hazardous waste and hazardous recyclable materials. It is reproduced from guidelines in *Export and Import of Hazardous Waste and Hazardous Recyclable Material Regulations—Guide to Hazardous Waste and Hazardous Recyclable Material Classification* published by the Government of Canada, specifically, Environment and Climate Change Canada. This passage is highly technical and aimed at a specialized audience.

2. Now visit the Hazardous Waste Home Page of the American Environmental Protection Agency (EPA) (https://www.epa.gov/hw), and navigate your way around the site to explore the information presented there in the link to hazardous waste regulations. The information available on the EPA website on hazardous waste has been written using principles of plain language, making it clear and accessible to a range of readers.

3. Using the information discussed in this chapter and in Chapter 4, "Writing Technical Prose," on plain language, analyze and make notes on which strategies the writers of the regulations on hazardous waste in the US have used to achieve their clear discussion. Which strategies are used most frequently? Which strategies do you think are most effective?

4. Based on your analysis of the plain language strategies used on the EPA website and the discussions on plain language in this book, rewrite the section reproduced in Figure 2.6 to make the regulations more easily accessible and comprehensible by employees in the Waste Management industry to classify oxidizing substances and organic peroxides. Your purpose in revising this passage is to help employees make classification decisions more easily and efficiently. If necessary, research some of the specific chemistry concepts and processes referred to in the *Guide* excerpt so that you can explain them for your non-specialist readers (e.g., "exothermic self-accelerating decomposition" or "compounds that contain oxygen in the bivalent '-O-O-' structure").

For more information or to find the complete *Guide*, visit the Environment and Natural Resources webpage of the Government of Canada.

Class 5: Oxidizing Substances and Organic Peroxides

Divisions

Class 5 has two divisions:

Class 5.1: Oxidizing Substances, which consists of substances that yield oxygen thereby causing or contributing to combustion of other material (as determined in accordance with section 2.5.2 of Chapter 2.5 of the UN Recommendations); and

Class 5.2: Organic Peroxides, which consists of substances that

(i) are thermally unstable organic compounds that contain oxygen in the bivalent "-O-O-" structure (as determined in accordance with section 2.5.3 of Chapter 2.5 of the UN Recommendations);

(ii) are liable to undergo exothermic self-accelerating decomposition;

(iii) have one or more of the following characteristics:

(A) liable to explosive decomposition

(B) burn rapidly

(C) sensitive to impact or friction

(D) react dangerously with other substances

(E) cause damage to the eyes; or

(iv) are in the list of currently assigned organic peroxides in section 2.5.3.2.4 of Chapter 2.5 of the UN Recommendations.

FIGURE 2.6

Excerpt on oxidizing substances from *Export and Import of Hazardous Waste and Hazardous Recyclable Material Regulations—Guide to Hazardous Waste and Hazardous Recyclable Material Classification*, Environment and Climate Change Canada Waste Reduction and Management Division (March 2017), 6–7.

MAJOR PROJECT 2.1

ETHICAL DILEMMA PAPER

This assignment requires you to connect ethical theories to positions you hold as a professional and as a citizen.[9]

Write a 500-word paper outlining an ethical theory and its application to an ethical dilemma. Follow these steps:

1. Select one of the following topics:

- Oil sands development—yes or no?
- Free post-secondary education for all—yes or no?

2. Clearly identify and use one of the following philosophical principles:

- Utilitarianism—John Stuart Mill
- Virtue Ethics—Aristotle
- Formalism—Immanuel Kant
- Contractarianism—John Rawls

3. Using the philosophical principle you have chosen, discuss the topic you have selected, exploring its ethical dimensions by outlining the issue at hand and then proposing a solution based on the chosen ethical principle. The idea is to show the reader how the application of your selected ethical theory helps us to make an ethical choice between the two options. The paper will be divided into two basic sections:

Part I: Identification and explication of the philosophical principle

Part II: Current ethical dilemma explained and "solved" (based on Part I)

At least two (2) properly cited references must be given at the end of the paper. One source should be directly related to the position you take on the dilemma you choose and the other should be related to your chosen philosophical principle.

9 Glen Thomas of the Mechanical Engineering department at the University of Alberta designed this position paper assignment for his Introduction to Mechanical Engineering course and has generously allowed us to include it here.

CHAPTER THREE

Researching Technical Subjects

Researching a subject in technical communication can be different from researching a subject in other areas. Your main source of information may be other people rather than books, so you may have to expand your research skills to include methods such as interviewing and surveying. These methods seek out information that is not published anywhere, nor is it available in document form. Information that you generate that has not been published before is called "primary research." Your efforts to record the information in your technical document may be the first time this information has been committed to print. In business workplaces, the information that is needed is often so specific or proprietary that it must be created by you—no published research exists that is specific enough for the problem you are trying to solve.

"Secondary research" refers to information that presents the findings of previously published research; if you find articles in the library or online, you are doing secondary research, but if you interview people and report what they said, you are doing primary research. Secondary research, such as literature reviews in academic documents or professional genres such as white papers, maps out what is already published about a topic. Academic writers often start their research projects by consulting the existing research (the secondary research). Once they identify "gaps" in the existing knowledge, they then do some primary research of their own to fill these gaps.

This chapter offers a concise review of three methods of information collection: interviewing subject matter experts, effective survey design, and finding and evaluating traditional print and online sources.

PRIMARY RESEARCH: INTERVIEWING

One important source of information for technical communicators documenting a new product or system is often the individuals who developed it. This information is gathered through interviewing—that is, meeting these individuals with a prepared list of questions to discuss aspects of the product or system, so you will be better able to write the operation or reference manual for it. Generally, the individuals who provide information about new technical products or systems are called "subject matter experts." Your role, as a technical communicator, is to be the intermediary between the subject matter experts' technical expertise and the users' relative lack of knowledge.

One of the best methods for gathering the information, then, is the interview. There are three stages to completing a successful interview:

- Preparing for it
- Conducting it
- Writing it up

PREPARING FOR THE INTERVIEW

Preparing yourself to conduct the interview is a crucial first step to increasing the chance that you create goodwill with the individual you interview and that you gather all or most of the information that you need. Prepare yourself in the following areas:

- Learn in advance everything that you can about the subject that you plan to discuss with the subject matter expert
- Learn in advance as much as you can about the person who is the subject matter expert
- Prepare a list of well-organized questions

Learn Everything You Can about the Subject

Read any documentation associated with the product or system that you will discuss with the subject matter expert in the interview. The greater your own technical knowledge about it, the better your chances are of understanding what it is you still need to learn, of formulating good questions that will elicit that information from your subject matter expert, and of understanding the answers from the expert in response to your questions. If you can discuss the new product or system using accurate terminology, you will develop credibility with your interviewee because he or she will see that you do have some knowledge of the subject matter.

Next, discover the **PURPOSE OF THE PRODUCT** or system. What will it enable one to do? Why is it better than other similar products? If you understand what can be done with the product or system, you can focus your research efforts on gathering the information that will help users accomplish their goals when they come to use the device.

Then, determine your **PURPOSE IN WRITING THE PLANNED DOCUMENT**. If your purpose is to persuade readers to buy this product, you will want to learn about and discuss during the interview the main advantages of your product over the competition's. If you are showing readers how to use a particular application, you need to assemble specific information about the actions required to accomplish various tasks.

In addition to reading about the item that you plan to document, you might also attend in-house training courses (if any are available) or obtain a copy of the product or system so that you can experiment with it. What questions does your use of the product raise for you that a subject matter expert might be able to answer? Use training courses as a way to make contact with individuals who know something about the product or system. Ask them whether you can contact them later with questions that they might answer.

All of these strategies will help you learn about the subject of your writing. The higher your level of knowledge, the fewer basic questions you need to ask, enabling you more easily to ferret out other important information to help you accomplish your purpose in writing the document.

Learn about the Subject Matter Expert

Before you schedule the interview, learn as much as you can about the subject matter expert. This means doing some research on her or him to find out about interests, specialties, and personality. Check out other projects he or she may have worked on. Ask co-workers about their experiences with this individual to give you some insight into what the individual is like to deal with one-on-one, but don't be influenced by other judgments, especially if they seem negative. You are collecting information to help you approach this person and motivate her or him to cooperate with you. Depending upon your attitude and approach, you may find him or her much more friendly and helpful than others report.

Prepare a List of Organized Questions

ORGANIZE AHEAD

Before you schedule the interview, prepare and organize your list of questions. That way, if the individual replies, "I'm not busy now; why don't you come over?" you will be able to say, "I'm on my way."

CREATE A LEGIBLE, NUMBERED LIST

Your list of questions should be written down, either typed or in legible handwriting, and numbered. The numbering also helps you to keep track of your questions and cross them off as they are answered. An ordered list also helps you to control and direct the interview, since your interview subject may not always want to talk about the same topics as you do. The list helps ensure that you gain the information you need about the topics that you think are important.

STRUCTURE THE QUESTIONS TO CONTROL THE INTERVIEW

Structure your questions so that there is a recognizable shape and progression to your interview. You might order them from general to more specific; you might move from discussion of basic functions of an application to more advanced features. This approach allows you to build on earlier information as well as ask impromptu questions that occur to you based on your interviewee's responses.

Organize your questions into a logical or topical progression to help you cover all necessary aspects of the subject. Ordering your questions according to the outline of your document can also help you when you begin writing, because you won't have to reorganize everything according to a different plan.

WRITE EXTRA QUESTIONS

Write more questions than you think necessary for the interview. This way, if your subject matter expert answers the questions clearly and efficiently, you won't run out of material before the interview is scheduled to end.

WRITING GOOD QUESTIONS

Good questions start with the six basic journalists' tools: who, what, where, when, why, and how. Use these to begin. As you explore the possibilities surrounding each word, more specific questions should occur to you.

Here are a few tips to help you develop questions that will give you the answers you need:

- Don't ask questions that can be answered by "yes" or "no."

Ask questions that require elaboration and explanation. If you were writing an operating manual for a computer application for novice users, which question would give you the most useful information?

1. Are the program's functions represented by icons that appear on every screen?
2. If a new user opened the program, where would he or she find information about the functions that can be performed?

The second version of this question is more likely to provide you with information that you don't already have.

- Ask questions that you cannot answer otherwise.

Once you gain access to your subject matter expert, ask questions that only he or she can answer. Your research should have generated some questions and issues for you that remain unanswered at this point: use your earlier notes and observations to help you generate such questions.

- Ask about topics that you don't understand.

Again, capitalize on the subject matter expert's knowledge by asking her or him to explain aspects of the product or system that you can't figure out.

- Include detail and background to your questions to help provide context.

Asking a question out of the blue can confuse your interviewee. As a preamble to the question, include background information that will orient your listener to the general topic and make it faster and more efficient for her or him to formulate an answer. If it becomes clear that the background is unnecessary, you can always skip over it.

- Ask what may seem to be "stupid" questions.

Finally, don't be afraid to ask what might appear to you to be obvious or stupid questions, if you really don't know the answer. Sometimes, such questions will quickly clear up fundamental misunderstandings. Other times, these are the questions that your users might ask, were they able to, questions that no one else has considered because answers seem so obvious to individuals who are experts on the topic.

CONDUCTING THE INTERVIEW

Once you have completed your research about the device or system you are documenting and you have organized your interview questions, next focus on the interview process itself. The following overview will start you thinking about how to prepare yourself to conduct a successful information-gathering session.

Schedule an Hour-Long Interview, If Possible

Contact the subject matter expert to schedule the interview. An appropriate length of time for the interview is usually one hour. You will probably find that an hour is about the maximum that you can remain alert, engaged, and sharp. After the hour passes, both you and your interviewee may become too tired to make efficient use of the time.

If your project requires several hours of discussion with the interviewee, then set up a series of meetings over several weeks rather than trying to complete your research in one session. Only schedule additional meetings if there is significant information that you still need to collect.

Introduce Yourself and Explain Your Project

When you call to schedule the interview, introduce yourself to the subject matter expert, explain your credentials, and describe the kind of information that you need. Explain why you believe he or she is the best source of this information, if it isn't immediately obvious.

Decide Whether to Record the Interview

To create a permanent record of the interviewee's responses, you will need to either record them or take detailed written notes (using a laptop computer or pen and paper). While an audio recording of the interview may seem useful, there are a few possible drawbacks to recording. First, you have to listen to or transcribe the conversation later. Listening in real time can slow down your progress. As for transcribing the audio files, numerous options for voice recognition software exist to convert your recording into written text. Search for "online transcription software" to find some of these options. Many programs offer free short (30-minute) trial usage of the program, which may be long

---

Prepare to Interview a Classmate

Prepare a list of questions to use in interviewing a classmate. Decide what general area of life you are interested in knowing more about and write a list of at least 10 questions that you might ask. Make sure that none of them can be answered by a simple "yes" or "no." Here are some suggestions for possible areas of inquiry:

- Plans for after graduation?
- Grad school?
- Work?
- Travel?
- Family history?
- Biographical information?
- Hobbies and/or interests?

enough to transcribe a recording for a school assignment. Second, some people object to having their interviews recorded, so ask permission before you begin recording. Third, recordings may fail (operator error turning it on, the recording-device battery runs down, etc.).

The advantages to recording are obvious: the interview can proceed more smoothly and naturally because the speaker doesn't have to wait while you scribble key points before proceeding with the explanation. You can maintain eye contact and think about the next question or decide that a follow-up question is needed. The information is recorded accurately, so you can later review specific points to clarify your understanding.

If you decide to record the interview, also take notes so that you can record the context of the speaker's comments as well as your impressions as the discussion continues.

If you decide to take notes exclusively, then, once the interview ends, you should review your notes immediately to add details and impressions that you remember but did not have time to record.

Be an Active Listener

As you conduct the interview, use ACTIVE LISTENING to respond to your interviewee's answers. Active listening is the practice of checking your understanding of the speaker's comments by rephrasing them to state what you think you heard. This rephrasing enables interviewees to verify that you have understood their point accurately and to correct any misperceptions.

Be aware of the nonverbal cues that you give your speaker as he or she talks. Try to make eye contact, even if you are taking notes, and smile and nod encouragingly to show that the information is helpful. Mannerisms that indicate positive interest will motivate your speaker to continue to talk, which is your goal.

Control the Interview

Sometimes, you may find your subject matter expert getting bogged down in minute technical details, which he or she finds fascinating but which do not help you to accomplish your task. In this case, you need to tactfully bring the speaker back to talking about the information that you can use. For example, you might point out that, while this particular explanation is fascinating, you would appreciate it if the speaker could also explain how it might tie into the information that the user needs to know.

Working with Those for Whom English Is a Second Language

Sometimes your subject matter expert will not have a good grasp of English. If he or she does not understand a question, then try rephrasing it to locate vocabulary that is familiar and will help clarify your point. You might also consider drawing sketches to illustrate the point or using the technology while the interviewee observes you and comments on your actions.

Closing the Interview

When your information is complete or the time scheduled for your interview has passed, wrap up the discussion. If you have unanswered questions, you may need to schedule a second interview. Thank your interviewee for talking with you, and make it clear that his or her answers have provided you with valuable information. If interviewees understand that you consider the time well spent, they will be more willing to talk with you again about later aspects of this project or another one. Arrange to have your subject matter expert answer any follow-up questions that might arise when you review your notes or convert responses into written text.

PRIMARY RESEARCH: CONDUCTING SURVEYS

Student evaluations generally take the form of surveys. Your experience in filling out those forms may have given you some insight into the limitations and advantages of survey methods: do the questions sometimes direct you to answer in a certain way? Is there enough time given to express your thoughts about the course and the instructor? Are you confident that the results will be kept confidential until the grades for the course have been submitted? Confidentiality, time limits, and loaded questions are just some of the limitations that may affect survey results. In this section of the chapter, we'll discuss some ways that you can avoid these problems while benefiting from the advantages of surveys: a large number of people can be consulted, the same questions are asked of each participant, and results can be quantified and compared to those from other surveys.

You may also have been asked by telemarketers to participate in survey research projects, and some may even have offered to pay you for the time it takes to participate in the survey. Not every research project has a budget to pay participants, though, and many good projects depend on the goodwill of participants to succeed. If you choose to do survey research or need to do survey research as part of your writing project, one thing you'll need to do is determine what would motivate people to participate in your survey.

Survey research can help you at two stages in your technical communication project: before you begin writing and as part of usability testing (revising). In the initial stages of the project, you could do surveys to find out what users are looking for in a manual: what are the tasks they do most often? What tasks confuse them the most? What are their most frequently used methods of solving a problem when they are using the software or device you are writing about? The answers to these kinds of questions could save you an enormous amount of time and effort if you get good information before you begin drafting your document.

ASKING GOOD QUESTIONS

Survey research is a method of generating information by asking questions of a large group of people. The quality of your survey, however, is directly related to your skill at asking good questions. There are two main types of questions to ask: closed-ended and open-ended. Closed-ended questions have the range of possible answers printed below the question itself; these questions are said to be closed because the range of answers is predetermined.

Kind of Question	Example
Closed-ended	How often did you contact your academic advisor when you were a student? 1. Never 2. Once or twice 3. Each academic term
Open-ended	What was the best advice you got from your academic advisor while you were a student?

FIGURE 3.1
Examples of open-ended and closed-ended survey questions.

Open-ended questions allow respondents to answer in their own words and to give some insight into why they think the way they do. They allow for unanticipated responses—and sometimes that is the most valuable information you can obtain from a survey! For example, you could ask a respondent "Why do you take/not take public transportation to school?" The range of possible answers could be quite wide, and the unanticipated answers could lead to innovative responses that would improve services. This wide range of answers also constitutes the biggest disadvantage to open-ended questions: the data are difficult to group into categories because the answers vary so much.

Closed-ended questions are more efficient for respondents: they can answer these questions quickly because the answers are right there for them.

> **What is the single most important reason that you avoid buying books at the campus bookstore?**
>
> 1. High prices
> 2. Long lines
> 3. No used copies are stocked
> 4. Other (please specify) _____

FIGURE 3.2
Example of a closed-ended question.

The data generated by closed-ended questions are more reliable (that is, the same question asked of the same person will almost always give the same resulting answer) and easier to code and compile into tables and statistics. These advantages may also cause problems: the predetermined categories might force respondents to choose an answer that does not accurately reflect what they think (that is, the answers may not be valid or an accurate measure of what respondents think). There may be a combination of reasons for avoiding the campus bookstore that the question in Figure 3.2 does not capture.

One final consideration involves time. In general, the longer it takes for respondents to complete a survey, the more likely it is that they will not finish it or return it to you. Open-ended questions take longer to answer than closed-ended ones, so limit your use of open-ended questions. Use open-ended questions to uncover the most important information you want to know.

GUIDELINES FOR ASKING GOOD QUESTIONS

Once you have decided which kinds of questions you want to ask, use the following guidelines to write the questions themselves:

- Rephrase jargon and technical language into plain language
- Ask specific questions
- Avoid loaded questions
- Break compound questions into individual questions

Rephrase Jargon and Technical Language into Plain Language
before:
Which database systems provide a variety of tools that allow specialized interfaces for tasks such as order entry and report generation to be constructed quickly?
better:
Which databases provide specialized interfaces to quickly enter information and generate reports?

Ask Specific Questions
before:
What do you do when you cannot determine where to click?
better:
When you are in the Build section of the WebCT/Vista interface, where do you click to return to the screen that shows how to enter student grades?

Avoid Loaded Questions
before:
Has your undergraduate advisor ever given you even a single piece of good advice?
better:
How would you characterize the quality of the advice that your undergraduate advisor has given you?

Break Compound Questions into Individual Questions
before:
Should the undergraduate student council sponsor more social events or lower the fees that they charge you?
better:
- Should the undergraduate student council sponsor more social events?
- Should the undergraduate student council lower the fees that they charge you?

CHOOSING APPROPRIATE RESPONSES

Asking good questions is only half of the challenge when you write questions. The other half is creating appropriate responses. Open-ended questions, of course, do not provide a structured response by the very nature of these questions. Responses to closed-ended questions can take one of the following forms:

- Yes/no answers
- Rating scales
- Comparative rating scales
- Category scales

YES/NO answers are, well, self-evident. Respondents can answer yes or no. The trick with these questions is to make sure that the situation you are asking about is really this black and white. Yes/no questions can also be organized into a list so that you can obtain quite a bit of information from one question:

1. Which of the following software applications have you used in the past year:
   ___ Microsoft Word
   ___ Excel
   ___ Photoshop®

RATING SCALES ask respondents to answer a question with a number that represents a response. The number they assign can vary; the following list offers some options:

- Pick one of the listed numerical responses
- Assign a number to the responses listed
- Choose among a range of numbers
- Select a number aligned with a word or phrase that describes the response each number corresponds to

FIGURE 3.3
Two examples of a Likert scale using five-point intervals. The first one provides a numbered list, the second a graphic representation with a numbered line.

Computer support in your workgroup is adequate:
1. Strongly disagree
2. Disagree
3. Neither agree nor disagree
4. Agree
5. Strongly agree

1	2	3	4	5
STRONGLY DISAGREE	DISAGREE	NEITHER AGREE NOR DISAGREE	AGREE	STRONGLY AGREE

The Likert scale is one such scale. The traditional one uses a five-point interval. These intervals can be represented either as a list or more graphically along a line with numbers. Figure 3.3 shows a Likert scale using a numbered list or a numbered line.

COMPARATIVE RATING scales differ by asking respondents to rank each of the responses in relation to the other ones. In one survey sent with a power tool, respondents were asked this question:

Using the numbers in the above list, indicate your three most important activities:
- ___ Golf
- ___ Camping
- ___ Avid book reading
- ___ Wildlife
- ___ Gambling

Apparently, the idea was to generate a comparative ranking in an attempt to determine whether any of these activities had a connection to buying power tools.

The last kind of response you could structure establishes **CATEGORIES** that respondents select. Instead of individual selections, you provide categories or ranges for respondents. Many people, if asked, could not say how many times in the past month they had used a particular software application, but they could reliably put themselves into a category that allowed them some margin of error: "frequently," "sometimes," or "almost never" are three categories that are often used to structure these answers.

PREPARING THE SURVEY FORM

Surveys can be done on paper, online, and on the phone. Whatever delivery method you choose, prepare the survey so it is clear, easy to read, and encourages your respondents to finish. Even telephone surveys need to have clearly written and well-designed forms for the caller to read to the survey respondent. How well you design your form will directly affect your success rate in obtaining completed survey forms.

Follow these guidelines as you prepare your form:

- Give the survey a title
- Briefly introduce your topic and motivate respondents to complete the survey
- Order the questions: start with easy or factual answers to suggest the survey will be quick to complete
- Leave plenty of space for respondents to answer open-ended questions
- Edit the survey; keep only the questions that you really need the answers to
- Leave lots of white space

CREATE A SURVEY FORM

- Create a survey form on computer lab usage to give to students who use the public labs on campus. Use the information in this section of the chapter to help you generate survey questions that tell you what you want to know about computer lab usage.
- Distribute the finished survey form and collect your data. You should get as many responses as you can (aim for 20 to 30 completed surveys).
- Tabulate and analyze your data. Create two or three visuals from the data that you could use in a written document summarizing the results of your survey.
- Write a memo or report that summarizes the data. Direct this report or memo to the administrators at your institution who would be interested in the responses of student users of the computer labs. If your goal is to argue for improved lab service (or maintenance or equipment updates), use the data to make an argument as to how the administration should respond to your survey.

Your memo or report should include at least one data table and one other type of visual that summarizes interesting points about your data. (See Chapter 5 for more information about using visuals.)

While the quality of your data matters, it is also important to determine what type of data you've collected. Open-ended questions result in QUALITATIVE data: data that cannot be counted easily but that can describe the qualities or details of an answer well. If you get repetitive answers to an open-ended question, treat them as quantitative and report them as numbers. As you read through the words that respondents have written, look for patterns and group similar responses. As you think about how to write your technical document, answers to these open-ended questions may help you understand how users will actually use the document, insights that might not come up in responses to closed-ended questions.

Closed-ended questions will give you answers to count: QUANTITATIVE data. For example, in answer to the question "What year of university study are you in?" students could have responded this way:

- First year: 2
- Second year: 11
- Third year: 7
- Fourth year: 4
- Other (please explain): 1 (student at large)

You would total these results on an unfilled-out copy of the survey, but, in your report based on this research, you might want to present the data in a table:

In your report, you might combine some of these data: 72 per cent of the students in this class are second- or third-year students, and very few first-year students enroll in it. What you are doing here is looking for patterns in the data to generalize what you are finding.

When collected in the initial stages of your project, survey findings can answer questions about the usefulness of the direction you plan to take. Based on the responses from your survey population, you can make adjustments early on or rest assured that your project is on track to provide the best document for your user group. When considered as part of usability testing, survey findings can reveal areas of the document that need revision, improved visuals, clarification of a point, or perhaps they can even highlight that the level of detail is too basic for your target user group.

Year of student	Number of responses	Percentage
First year	2	8
Second year	11	44
Third year	7	28
Fourth year	4	16
Other	1	4

FIGURE 3.4

In a report, present data in a table for easy reference for readers.

REPORTING SURVEY DATA

Once you have produced your survey, you need to distribute it. For a quick informal survey, you will probably distribute it to a wide range of people. If you are doing more serious work, you must decide what group of people you are surveying and how many of those people you can afford to contact. Then you track how many of the people that you selected to survey actually filled in and returned the survey form: this is called the response rate (the percentage of people who responded). The higher the response rate, the stronger your data will be.

SECONDARY RESEARCH: LIBRARIES AND OTHER ONLINE SOURCES

Libraries are better stocked with useful sources and information than ever before both in print and in digital form. The key advantage of libraries (versus online search engines) is that they are CURATED: large staffs of people take great care to weed out unreliable sources. Search engines such as Google do not offer that advantage.

CONDUCTING AN EFFECTIVE SEARCH FOR SOURCES: LIBRARY AND INTERNET

When you need to find some sources, you want them to be the most relevant and useful to your topic. Finding the most useful information depends largely on the keywords that you select to use in your search. If you don't use the appropriate technical terms, then your search won't locate useful publications.

To improve the chances that you will name your subject matter correctly in the search, generate a list of words that you associate with the topic. Then, list as many synonyms for each word as you can think of. If your list is a bit short, you could also consult web search site subject directories (e.g., Yahoo!® Directory, Google® Directory, or The Library of Congress's RefSeek Reference Directory). A subject directory can help you think of subcategories related to your broader topic. You can also browse or use keyword searches at the library. Browsing allows you to search by author, title, or assigned library subject heading when you already know some of the main sources to use. Keyword searches allow you to access related information from databases. You can also mine some of the sources that your initial searches turn up for additional keywords related to your subject. Other options are to consult a specialized dictionary on your topic or the Library of Congress subject headings (for example, authorities.loc.gov), since most educational libraries use the Library of Congress Subject Headings to organize their holdings.

Once you have generated a respectable list of keywords, you will find that, if you enter just one word, the sources that you locate will be too diffuse and general for actual usefulness. To narrow your search, you may need to combine two or three keywords (using AND) to focus and qualify the sources that show up on your screen. You may also be able to narrow your search by specifying what you don't want (e.g., **NOT** crystalline semiconductors). Some search engines simplify this process by allowing you to use a plus or minus in front of the term to indicate combining and excluding (e.g., +amorphous semiconductors –crystalline semiconductors). Others provide access to advanced search options such as this on a separate page.

When you have located several useful sources, you can also study their reference sections to locate additional information relevant to your topic. Often, a useful article will contain references to other useful articles on the same or a related subject.

If you have difficulty finding useful sources on your own, visit the library and ask a reference librarian to help you. Librarians can shortcut your search time by directing you to the right subject headings, and they can also suggest the location of various types of sources in the building. They can help you efficiently locate some useful material.

ASSESSING THE CREDIBILITY OF YOUR SOURCES

Once you locate what look like relevant and useful books, articles, and websites, assess their reliability and credibility. Especially for website-based information, the credibility of the source must be sound. Anyone can put up a website, and no one polices the accuracy or legitimacy of the information posted. Some websites even pretend to credibility and distinction by imitating the look of respected websites posted by well-known organizations or governments. Look closely at the **URL** and other details to make sure you are visiting the legitimate site.

Credibility of Print Sources

Here is a list of the criteria that librarians use to assess printed material:

1. **PUBLISHER**: Who published the document? Scholarly books and journal articles are reviewed by experts in the area before they are published. If the document is scholarly (from a university press, for example), it is likely fairly reliable: it has been screened for accuracy and reliability. If it appears in a popular magazine or book, it may be less reliable because the selection criteria in such sources are based more on interest and entertainment than accuracy or thoroughness.

2. **AUTHOR**: Who wrote the document? What are this person's qualifications in this area? Does the author have a professional degree or connection with the subject matter that is legitimate and sanctioned by related professional organizations?

3. **CURRENCY**: How recent is the document? If the topic is a hot one, such as artificial intelligence, then it matters how recently the source was published. An article or book that is several years old may be out of date since developments in artificial intelligence are ongoing, and the field changes rapidly in a very short time.

4. **EVIDENCE:** What is the basis of the information presented? Did the author conduct interviews, experiments, observations, etc. to gather the evidence he or she uses to support the claims? Does the author cite relevant and current research and provide proper documentation, so you can find this material yourself? Is enough evidence presented to support the claims?

5. **SLANT:** Can you figure out areas where the writer seems biased in the opinions expressed? To what extent might these biases affect the information presented?

Depending upon how you answer the questions posed in the list above, you can evaluate the credibility of a particular print source on a scale from useful and relevant to biased and unsupported. Then you can decide whether to include the information in your document or continue to search for other material with more trustworthy content.

Credibility of Online Sources

The criteria that you can use to evaluate the credibility of an Internet or website source are similar to those useful for evaluating print sources, but some of the criteria will be impossible to verify on the website. In this case, you should probably keep searching for a source that you can verify as accurate and reputable rather than use a source that may be unreliable. Here are some questions that will help you evaluate a website's credibility:

1. **WEBSITE SPONSOR:** What type of URL does the site use? Is it a government site (ending in .gov or .gc.ca)? Is it a commercial site (ending in .com)? Is it a non-profit site (ending in .org)? Is it a university or college-sponsored site (ending in .edu, sometimes, or sometimes just .ca in Canada or .au in Australia)? The final tag on the website URL can give you some indication of whether or not the site is sponsored by a reputable organization. Government and educational websites tend to sponsor information that is more reliable and accurate than many commercial websites, which have as their goal selling a service or product.

2. **AUTHOR:** Who has written the information that you want to use? Often websites don't identify authors beyond giving their email address. Without at least a name, you may have difficulty assessing the qualifications of the writer, and therefore the validity of the opinions or information that he or she has published.

3. **CURRENCY:** Does the website have a date and time when the information was posted or last updated? Many websites do provide this detail, but others do not. If you cannot verify the currency of the posting, then you should keep searching for a source that you know is current, especially if timeliness of information is a goal.

4. **EVIDENCE**: Many websites do not clarify the source of their information, so you may have difficulty verifying their level of accuracy. Look for some idea of who or what organization is sponsoring the website ("About Us"). You can evaluate the accuracy and reliability of its content based on who is affiliated with the website. If the site does not have an obvious reputable sponsor, or does not identify the sources for the information it presents, you should probably stay away because you cannot verify its reliability.

5. **SLANT**: While some websites are overtly political or slanted in their views, others cloak their bias by sounding reasonable and scientific. They may cite statistics as evidence of their claims, but unless you can evaluate the origin of their data, you cannot really tell whether information is legitimate or fabricated.

6. **ADVERTISING**: Watch for sites whose main purpose is to sell you a service or product. Many sites exist solely to promote the sale of something, and any information they contain will be as reliable as any advertising.

When you have located enough reliable and useful sources, you can begin using them to develop your own document. Reputable sources and statistics can help you build a solid case for the argument you want to make or help you feel confident about the quality of the technical information that you are presenting. The main challenge of integrating research sources into your text is ensuring that you paraphrase or cite them properly. The next section briefly reviews the difference between quoting and paraphrasing and how to highlight the original source to keep your readers informed as to the source of your research materials.

SUMMARIZING AND CITING RESEARCHED SOURCES

One of the significant differences between writing in science and engineering and writing in humanities-based disciplines is the use of quotations, paraphrase, and summary. Writers in humanities disciplines such as English studies or philosophy are permitted—expected, even—to use **QUOTATIONS** (reproducing exactly a passage from a relevant source) to succinctly express the cited author's ideas. Otherwise, they paraphrase their sources. However, in science and technical disciplines, writers may not quote, and they use paraphrase sparingly. Instead they **SUMMARIZE** and **CITE** sources.

Figure 3.5 is an excerpt from a review article in *Food and Function*, a journal published by the Royal Society of Chemistry, which uses CSE style. The author, David McClements, neither quotes from his sources nor paraphrases them. Rather, he lays out his argument and inserts numbers that indicate the sources that form its basis.

REDUCING CALORIE DENSITY.

One of the major factors contributing to diet-related problems in developed countries is the overconsumption of calorie-dense foods, such as cookies, cakes, snacks, and breads, which are rich in digestible fats and carbohydrates.[5-7] There has therefore been growing interest in developing reduced-calorie versions of these foods so that consumers can still enjoy them, but experience fewer adverse health effects.[8-10] The development of these kinds of products relies on knowledge of the molecular/physicochemical basis of food quality and deliciousness.[1,11] In particular, the way that specific food ingredients and structures contribute to the desirable appearance, aroma, taste, sound, and feel of foods is required. This knowledge can then be used to reformulate foods to reduce the levels of high-calorie ingredients (such as fat and starch), while maintaining their desirable sensory attributes. This is an important area that research scientists with expertise in structural design principles can contribute. A few selected examples of the kinds of approach that can be used to develop reduced-calorie foods are given here to highlight the science involved.

Digestible fats have twice the calorie density of digestible proteins and carbohydrates, which makes them an important target for the creation of reduced-calorie foods.[8] For this reason, many researchers have focused on the development of reduced-fat versions of common foods, like dressings, sauces, spreads, and baked goods. These products have to be designed to look, feel, and taste like the conventional versions, otherwise consumers will not purchase them and incorporate them into their diets. This aim can often be achieved using structural design principles to create food compositions and structures with the desired attributes. As an example, mayonnaise is an oil-in-water (O/W) emulsion that consists of a high concentration of oil droplets (typically > 70%) dispersed within a watery medium.[12] The desirable textural attributes of this kind of product, such as its spoonability, are the result of the fact that the fat droplets are packed so closely together that they cannot easily flow past each other when a force is applied. The fat content of this kind of product can be reduced using water in oil-in-water (W/O/W) emulsions. This kind of multiple emulsion can be designed to have a similar appearance, texture, and mouthfeel as a conventional mayonnaise but with a significantly lower fat and calorie content.[13] The fat content is reduced by incorporating small water droplets within the fat droplets (W/O), so that some of the fat is replaced by water (Fig. 2). This technology has already been used commercially to successfully produce reduced-calorie mayonnaise products that look, feel, and taste like the conventional versions, which are available in Japan.

Note that McClements indicates the sources for points he makes that are based on the work of others: for example, "There has ... been growing interest in developing reduced-calorie versions of these foods so that consumers can still enjoy them, but experience fewer adverse health effects.[8-10]" The numbers 8–10 inform readers that references 8, 9, and 10 are articles that discuss the development of healthier versions of consumers' favorite high calorie foods. The sentence that follows narrows the paragraph subject matter to "the molecular/physicochemical basis of food quality and deliciousness," and cites references 1 and 11 to support his point that chemistry can identify what makes food delicious. McClements then discusses his own ideas about the importance of "expertise in structural design principles" in creating these lower-calorie versions of food. He does not quote his references, nor does he paraphrase any specific ideas from these sources. Instead they form the backdrop against which his review of research in the field unfolds.

When you are locating your sources, don't forget to record all of the publication data carefully so that you can cite all sources accurately and completely, should you decide to use them.

·FIGURE 3.5

Passage from a review article in *Food and Function* that illustrates how to summarize and cite references using Council of Science Editors (CSE) number style.

Source: David Julian McClements, "Future Foods: A Manifesto for Research Priorities in Structural Design of Foods." Food and Function 11 (March 06, 2020): 1933–1945. https://doi.org/10.1039/c9fo02076d.

How do you know when you should cite sources? Here is a list of types of information that you should always cite:

- Statements of opinion
- Claims that can be argued
- Sources for statistics
- Research findings
- Examples
- Graphs
- Charts
- Illustrations

One type of information that you don't have to cite is facts, if they are widely known and readily available in general reference works such as an encyclopedia. For example, you would not need to document the fact that 0 degrees C is equal to 32 degrees F.

CHAPTER FOUR

Writing Technical Prose

CLARITY, COHESION, CONCISION

This chapter contains tips and strategies for improving the quality of your technical prose. You should aim to develop a clear and concise style that you can adapt to meet your readers' expectations. The first part of this chapter focuses on this concept of reader expectation. It identifies strategies for placing your key ideas where readers expect to find them and for linking ideas together logically to ensure that the interpretation readers create based on your text comes close to the meaning that you intended to communicate while writing. These strategies are grouped under two categories: clarity and cohesion. The second part of this chapter outlines methods for producing direct, effective, and concise technical prose.

CLARITY

Technical and scientific prose, because of its often-specialized subject matter, can be difficult to write clearly. At least, readers of technical and scientific prose can have difficulty understanding it—what the writer means is not at all clear—because they don't just "read" it, they interpret it. That is, as they read they derive clues from the prose structure to identify what appear to be the writer's main ideas. Readers assemble these ideas into a coherent pattern from which they construct the meaning of the sentence. They draw links between the main ideas that they have identified from sentence to sentence through a paragraph and from paragraph to paragraph through the text to build an understanding of what the document is "about." Understanding where readers look to find these clues can help you to situate the main ideas of your text in those places to help readers come closer to interpreting your meaning correctly.

Place the Context or the Familiar Information on the Left

Readers of English read from left to right, starting in the upper left corner and reading down to the bottom right corner of a page. For this reason, readers of English look to the left side for familiarity: they expect to see certain types of information on the left (e.g., the beginning of the page or the start of a sentence). They expect to see the context on the left, and the new information (that they need to interpret) on the right. If you meet reader expectations for where important information will appear, readers will find your prose clear.

Table 4.1 shows the parts of a formal definition, the term on the left side, the class in the middle, and the features on the right side. Readers look to the left column for information about the term being defined; as they read across the table, they expect each column to provide a bit more detailed information about the term. Readers experience this order for the information as clear because it leads them from the general to the specific, from the familiar to the new, from the context (what is an LED?) to the details to be discovered (the LED's specific features).

Term	Class	Features
LED	Semiconductor	Light bulb without a filament Doesn't get hot
Saturated fat	Fats from animals	Solid at room temperature Liquid when heated

TABLE 4.1

Place Main Ideas as the Subjects of Sentences

English sentences are usually structured with the subject first (in the left half of the sentence), followed by the verb (at the beginning of the right half of the sentence). Readers expect the subject of a sentence to hold a main idea; whatever you place in the subject position of a sentence will be regarded as important. If you bury the main idea in a dependent clause in the middle of the sentence rather than positioning it as the subject, readers will miss the fact that it's a main idea. Instead they will see the subject of the sentence (the first part) as being important.

In both versions shown in Figure 4.1, the subjects of each sentence are highlighted in red. In the first version, a quick scan over the subjects shows several different topics, some of which are main ideas in the paragraph (*another method*) and some which are not (*different researchers*). The subjects shift back and forth between researchers, methods, and details of the methods, so that it's difficult to determine the main topic in each sentence and to which part readers should pay the most attention.

EXAMPLE 1.1

In the past, **DIFFERENT RESEARCHERS** have used a variety of techniques to deposit a film or coating on a substrate located in a vacuum chamber. **RESEARCHERS** permitted the vapor, created through thermally vaporizing or evaporating a metal, to condense and be deposited on the substrate. **CHEMICAL VAPOR DEPOSITION** is another method wherein different gases introduced into the chamber react to form a compound on the substrate. Yet **ANOTHER METHOD** used by scientists is sputtering. **A CATHODE**, located inside a vacuum or gas-filled discharge tube, is disintegrated by bombardment until **IT** is vaporized and deposited on the substrate.

EXAMPLE 1.2

In the past, **VARIOUS TECHNIQUES** have been used to deposit a film or coating on a substrate located in a vacuum chamber. **ONE TECHNIQUE** simply is to thermally vaporize or evaporate a metal, permitting the vapor to condense and be deposited on the substrate. **ANOTHER TECHNIQUE** is referred to as chemical vapor deposition wherein different gases are introduced into the vacuum chamber to react and form a compound on the substrate. A third **TECHNIQUE** is referred to as sputtering. In this method, a vacuum or gas filled **DISCHARGE TUBE** has a cathode that is disintegrated by bombardment, so that **THE CATHODE MATERIAL** is vaporized and deposited on the substrate.

FIGURE 4.1
Placing
main ideas
as subjects.

In the second version, the central ideas are placed in the subject position of each sentence. A quick scan over the paragraph helps readers to see immediately that this paragraph is about a variety of techniques for coating substrates. The list of techniques is described such that readers can identify each one because each one is named and its distinguishing features highlighted ("another method is ... chemical vapor deposition wherein different gases are introduced").

Whatever appears at the beginning of a sentence creates for readers a context or perspective for understanding the sentence as a "unit." Readers expect that what appears in the subject position is what the story is about. Pay attention to what appears at the beginning of your sentences. Ensure that your subjects are nouns that represent and clarify your main ideas.

Locate the Subject and the Verb Close to One Another

Readers also expect that the subject of a sentence and its verb will be located close to one another. As readers process your sentence, they tend to suspend interpretation until after they've read **BOTH** the subject and the verb. If you have a long subordinate clause or series of phrases between the subject and its verb, readers will view these constructions as interruptions between the central parts of the sentence. Most readers view the subject as incomplete without its verb, and the point of the sentence is not clear to readers until they can put the subject and verb together. Any ideas located in the interrupting portion of the sentence are viewed as subordinate to the main point expressed in the subject and verb.

In Example 2.1 (see Figure 4.2), readers miss what the method is for while they wait for the verb at the end of the sentence. This construction actually de-emphasizes the description of the method, which is, in fact, the essential information that readers need to understand the sentence.

In Example 2.2, the subject and verb are adjacent with the important information located at the sentence end.

IN-CLASS EXERCISE 4.1

Place Main Ideas as the Subjects of Sentences

Rewrite the following paragraph to place the main ideas of each sentence in the subject position.

This analysis found that parity and smoking during pregnancy were significant contributors to the adiposity, defined as the weight/length ratio, while the main analysis did not find that these factors contributed to infant LGA (large for gestational age) classification. Also, antidepressant use was found to contribute to LGA classification but not to infant adiposity. These results suggest that the factors contributing to increased foetal adiposity may be subtly different from those contributing to LGA status. This has important implications for future work in this area, as LGA is often used as a proxy for excess infant adiposity.

IN-CLASS EXERCISE 4.2

Rewrite a Paragraph from Your Own Prose

Rewrite a paragraph that you've written as part of an assignment for your technical communication class making sure that the main ideas appear in the subject position in the sentences.

EXAMPLE 2.1

1. **A METHOD** for the reactive plating of substrates to produce transparent conducting films and photoactive coatings **IS DISCLOSED**.

EXAMPLE 2.2

2. **A METHOD IS DISCLOSED** for the reactive plating of substrates to produce transparent conducting films and photoactive coatings.

FIGURE 4.2
Placing subjects and verbs together.

Position Subjects and Verbs

Rewrite the following sentences so that the subject and verb are located together.

1. Prenatal Health Project recruiters were notified when women who fulfilled the eligibility criteria for the study had ultrasound appointments.
2. To determine if participants knowing they had gestational diabetes at the time of interview affected the results of this analysis, the more exclusive definition of gestational diabetes, which only included women who developed it after the interview, was used in this analysis.
3. Many of the errors that directly resulted in low yields would be eliminated had the experimenter been familiar with the separatory funnel, the physical appearance of the drying agent after all of the water present in the sample had been absorbed, and the speed with which diethyl ether evaporates.
4. This lack of inter-rater reliability was a fatal flaw of this exam, and, in the 1950s, the English Composition Test was discontinued and its replacement by a multiple-choice test of usage and mechanics was instituted.
5. Electrochemical methods are used to graft polymers chemically to metal surfaces, but, in general, organic molecules covalently bound to metals are less prevalent.

Place Important Ideas at the End of Sentences to Emphasize Them

The end of the sentence is also a point of emphasis—that is, as readers reach the close of the sentence, they expect the last few words to be significant to justify their effort reading to the end. In fact, based on this expectation, they will place significance upon whatever information you place in this point of emphasis.

In Figure 4.3, examine the phrases at the end of each main clause in Example 3.1 (the sentence marked with numbers 3 and 4 consists of two main clauses). To what extent does the information contained in red typeface reflect important information in the clause and in the paragraph? In most cases in this paragraph, the writer misses the opportunity to place an important idea in the position of emphasis at the end of the sentences. Clause 6 does locate an important idea in the paragraph—insulin resistance—in this position of emphasis.

In Example 3.2, we have revised the paragraph to emphasize the important information at the end of each lexical unit or sentence.

Readers place value on the information at the end of the sentence and then work to build a context around that material. If it's not important, they will misunderstand your writing because they are focusing on the wrong information. You placed it in a position of emphasis when it was not important. Readers also expect the information toward the end of the sentence to have logical links with information you have supplied earlier. Place new information toward the end of the sentence, after the verb. Your readers will create logical links between the earlier, familiar information and the new information toward the end of the sentence.

Use the ends of your sentences as places where you locate information you want to emphasize.

Place One Point in Each Syntactic Structure (That Is, a Unit Containing a Subject and Verb)

In Figure 4.4, example 4 reproduces an abstract from a physics experimental report. Even if you can't follow the technical subject matter, you can still identify the main ideas because each sentence or clause contains one point. Even the longest sentence still contains only one main idea: "MECHANICALLY STABLE POLYCRYSTALLINE conducting ZnO films having a preferred orientation WERE DEPOSITED WITH RESISTIVITIES in the range from 4.0×10^{-6} to 9.0×10^{-6} Ω m, WITH CARRIER DENSITIES of more than 2×10^{26} m^{-3} AND HALL MOBILITIES between 2.8×10^{-3} and 4.0×10^{-3} m^2 V^{-1} s^{-1}."

EXAMPLE 3.1

[1] Obesity is increasing at unprecedented rates WORLDWIDE (Seidell, 2000; Lu et al., 2001). [2] This increase suggests that more women than ever are entering pregnancy obese and that the incidence of pregnancy complications related to obesity IS INCREASING (Henrikson, 2006). [3] The combined degree of insulin resistance caused by pregnancy and obesity is greater than that for a NORMAL PREGNANCY, and, [4] as a result, the risk of gestational diabetes IS HIGHER. [5] It is more likely that, with a greater degree of insulin resistance, the beta cells (cells that produce insulin) will be unable to compensate, and hyperglycaemia WILL DEVELOP (Kahn, Hull, & Utzschneider, 2006). [6] It remains unclear whether increased insulin resistance precedes beta-cell dysfunction in the development of gestational diabetes or beta-cell dysfunction precedes INSULIN RESISTANCE (Catalano, 2002). [7] Most studies of gestational diabetes stratify risk and plasma glucose concentration measurements by weight based on the differences in insulin resistance that occur AS OBESITY INCREASES (Catalano, 2002).

EXAMPLE 3.2

[1] Obesity is increasing worldwide at UNPRECEDENTED RATES (Seidell, 2000; Lu et al., 2001). [2] This increase suggests that more women than ever are entering pregnancy obese, simultaneously leading to an increase in obesity-related PREGNANCY COMPLICATIONS (Henrikson, 2006). [3] Normal pregnancy represents a small RISK OF INSULIN RESISTANCE; however, [4] combined pregnancy and obesity increases the risk of insulin resistance, increasing the risk of developing GESTATIONAL DIABETES. [5] It is more likely that, with a greater degree of insulin resistance, beta cells (cells that produce insulin) will be unable to compensate, causing the DEVELOPMENT OF HYPERGLYCAEMIA (Kahn, Hull, & Utzschneider, 2006). It remains unclear in the development of gestational diabetes whether increased insulin resistance PRECEDES BETA-CELL DYSFUNCTION or [6] beta-cell dysfunction precedes INSULIN RESISTANCE (Catalano, 2002). [7] Most studies of gestational diabetes focus on the differences in insulin resistance that occur as obesity increases, so they stratify risk and plasma GLUCOSE CONCENTRATION MEASUREMENTS BY WEIGHT (Catalano, 2002).

FIGURE 4.3
Placing important ideas in the position of emphasis.

EXAMPLE 4

Abstract

Highly transparent conducting ZnO FILMS HAVE BEEN DEPOSITED using ion-beam-assisted reactive vacuum deposition. The zinc DEPOSITION RATE WAS CONTROLLED by adding gallium to the zinc in an open Al_2O_3 crucible source. OXYGEN WAS INTRODUCED into the system via a separate controlled leak AND REACTED with the zinc on the substrate. Mechanically stable polycrystalline conducting ZnO FILMS having a preferred orientation WERE DEPOSITED with resistivities in the range from 4.0×10^{-6} to 9.0×10^{-6} Ω m, with carrier densities of more than 2×10^{26} m^{-3} and Hall mobilities between 2.8×10^{-3} and 4.0×10^{-3} m^2 V^{-1} s^{-1}. The AVERAGE TRANSMISSION EXCEEDED 90% for films 350 nm thick in the wavelength range of the visible spectrum.

FIGURE 4.4
Placing one main idea in each clause or sentence.

Place Old Information That Links Back in the Subject Position, and Put New Information That You Want Readers to Attend to at the Point of Emphasis

All of your sentences are going to be structured from a series of familiar and new information. You can't, however, structure your sentences by rote always putting old information as the subject and new information at the conclusion because what falls in between will likely also be a blend of old and new

EXAMPLE 5.1

[1] The detail with which the variables were collected, especially for alcohol and tobacco use, per day as well as type of alcohol, was a major strength of this study. [2] This detail allowed for more precise estimates of the effects of alcohol on esophageal cancer. [3] The detailed data about age and tobacco consumption were combined with information from previous studies within the literature to produce a model that adequately controls for confounding by these factors. [4] Another strength of this analysis was its ability to tease apart the effects of different alcohol types. [5] Previous studies have been limited by the distribution of types within the population they were studying, which limited the inferences that could be drawn (Bosetti, 2000).

EXAMPLE 5.2

[1] A MAJOR STRENGTH of this study was *the detail* with which **the variables** were collected, especially for alcohol and tobacco use, per day as well as type of alcohol. [2] *This detail* allowed for more **precise estimates** of the effects of alcohol on esophageal cancer. [3] Using **data on age and tobacco consumption** and from previous studies from the literature, a **model** was produced that adequately controls for **confounding by these factors**. [4] ANOTHER STRENGTH of this analysis was its ability to *tease apart the effects of different alcohol types*. [5] *The distribution of types within the population being studied* has limited the inferences that could be drawn in previous studies (Bosetti, 2000).

FIGURE 4.5
Linking familiar and unfamiliar information to establish context.

IN-CLASS EXERCISE 4.4

Place Key Ideas in Positions of Emphasis

Revise the following sentences to place key ideas at the end.

1. Gestational diabetes occurs when maternal insulin secretion does not increase enough to maintain balanced plasma glucose concentrations throughout pregnancy, as insulin resistance increases.

2. Maternal BMI, pregnancy weight gain, total kilocalories consumed, and grams of omega-3 fatty acid consumed per day differed only slightly between women who developed gestational diabetes and those who did not; however, no statistical tests were performed.

3. Therefore, if a nondeterministic finite automaton can be constructed for the shuffle of two regular languages from the deterministic finite automata of those regular languages, then the class of regular languages under shuffle is closed.

4. My project management skills were enhanced by acting as lead Research Assistant on a study concerning the psychosocial aspects of pain, for which I coordinated and developed the research plan.

information. Instead, pay attention to the needs of readers by putting old information that links backward into the subject position. This helps readers put the ideas into context. And put new ideas that you want readers to remember toward the end of the sentence.

Example 5.1, in Figure 4.5, is a paragraph drawn from a biostatistical analysis of the effect that alcohol consumption has on the risk of developing esophageal cancer. This paragraph is difficult to read, in part, because of the tangled structure of the sentences. For example, "the detail with which the variables were collected" is the idea in the subject or topic position, which readers will reasonably expect to be the main point of the paragraph because of this placement. "The detail" does continue to be the main topic over three sentences until the focus shifts to "another strength of this analysis."

In Example 5.2, some sentences have been restructured to link the new ideas more clearly with the familiar information that establishes a context. Sentence 1 has been turned around so that "a major strength" is the main organizing topic to start. "The detail" then becomes an aspect of the strengths of the study, which the paragraph discusses. Sentence 2 links its point about precise estimates to the degree of detail in the data. Sentence 3 draws on the degree of detail again but to evaluate the confounders that were controlled in the model the research team developed. The fourth sentence elaborates a third strength of the study in the details related to the different types of alcohol examined. The fifth sentence notes that other studies have been limited by the lack of differentiation between the types of alcohol consumed by studied participants, a final statement about the quality of the analysis described. The revision in Example 5.2 shows how information familiar to readers is used to link new ideas back to established ideas to build a context that gives new ideas meaning.

Use Verbs Rather Than Nominalizations to Express Action in Your Sentences

Readers expect the subject of a sentence to contain some kind of actor that the story is about. In the paragraph in Example 5.2, "the study," "the detail in the variables," and "the distribution of types in the data" are the main actors in the paragraph (that is, the actors performing the action). Readers equally expect that the action taking place in a sentence will be expressed in the verb chosen to complete the subject. When the verbs in a paragraph do not contain the main actions, readers have no structural information about where those actions are described. This leads them to guess what the actions are.

EXAMPLE 6.1

[1] This trial WILL INVOLVE the process of construct validation, with the ultimate goal of contributing knowledge to the validity of the interpretations that ARE MADE on the basis of the exam mark. [2] An assessment of the true validity of the exam and the inferences drawn from it WOULD NEED TO HAVE a wider focus than looking at a single class offered (Weigle, 2002). [3] This type of assessment WOULD NEED TO LOOK more at the implications of the grades given in the course, which COULD BE DONE with an exam that HAS already BEEN SHOWN to measure what it WAS INTENDED to measure (Weigle, 2002). [4] This trial IS the first step toward a trial of the validity of inferences about how exam scores ARE USED, which MAY BE possible in the future.

EXAMPLE 6.2

[1] This trial EXAMINES the process of constructing validity. [2] The process ultimately AIMS to contribute knowledge to HELP instructors INTERPRET grades validly based on students' exam marks. [3] To assess the true validity of the exam and to draw inferences from it, we SHOULD BROADEN the focus of the trial beyond looking at a single class (Weigle, 2002). [4] This type of assessment also MUST EXAMINE the implications of the grades given in the course, which a proven exam COULD DO, one that MEASURES what it was intended to measure (Weigle, 2002). [5] This trial CONSTITUTES the first step toward a trial of the validity of inferences about how exam scores ARE USED, which MAY BE POSSIBLE in the future.

In Example 6.1 (see Figure 4.6), the verbs in the paragraph are highlighted in red (*will involve, are made, would need to have, would need to look, could be done, has been shown, was intended, is, are used, may be*). We cannot determine what actions are taking place based on these verb choices. Most are static verbs that declare states of being or possess characteristics rather than actions (*will involve, would need to have, has been shown*).

In sentence 1 of Example 6.1, the central point of the study is buried in a series of noun constructions or nominalizations: "the ultimate goal of contributing knowledge to the validity of the *interpretations*." If we extract the action from the nouns, we get this statement: "This trial ultimately aims to contribute

FIGURE 4.6
Using verbs to express the main actions.

IN-CLASS EXERCISE 4.5

Locate the Verbs in a Series of Nominalizations

Rewrite the paragraph below to extract the verbs that are hidden in the nominalizations. Then replace any static verbs with descriptive verbs that convey the action.

Using liquid-liquid *extraction*, molecule *separation* has *occurrence* through the *dissolution* of the compounds in an organic solvent and then the *acidification* or *basification* of the solution. This process results in the *creation* of water-soluble salt, which then causes *separation* from the organic layer. Any compound that failed in the formation of a water-soluble salt with the *addition* of the acid or base is still present in the organic layer. Depending on the properties of the molecules under *separation*, additional *separation* is possible from the organic layer. Acidic and basic compounds can achieve separate removal from the neutral compound, despite the *maintenance* of *dissolution* in the organic solvent.

FIGURE 4.7
Linking sentences from start to start.

knowledge to help enable instructors to *interpret* grades validly based on the exam mark."

In Example 6.2, the verbs in this passage have been revised to highlight the actions being performed. Not all of the verbs need to be revised for clarity; however, adding more descriptive verbs does help readers determine the actions that are being performed in the clinical trial. In the case of sentence 2, adding a descriptive verb also requires inserting the agent of the action, which helps to make the idea even clearer.

COHESION

Another strategy that significantly improves the clarity of scientific or technical communication is the effective use of cohesion. Attention to cohesion helps readers interpret meaning; they experience the writing as much clearer because ideas are clearly linked from one sentence to the next.

There are two methods of achieving cohesion:

- Linking sentences from start to start
- Linking sentences from end to start

Linking Sentences from Start to Start

Use familiar information at the start of each sentence to link ideas from one to the next throughout a paragraph. Example 7 (see Figure 4.7) uses this coherence strategy effectively. Each sentence describes a different method of producing thin films. At the end of the paragraph, readers have a clear overview of past methods.

Note that the writer in Example 7 shifts his terms slightly from "technique" to "method" over the paragraph. Be wary of changing your terms when using this coherence strategy unless it is clear to readers that the new term is a synonym for the earlier term. If the change in terminology confuses readers, your efforts at clarity will be wasted.

EXAMPLE 7

In the past, **VARIOUS TECHNIQUES** have been used to deposit a film or coating on a substrate located in a vacuum chamber. **ONE TECHNIQUE** simply is to vaporize or evaporate a metal thermally, permitting the vapor to condense and be deposited on the substrate. **ANOTHER METHOD** is referred to as chemical vapor deposition wherein different gases are introduced into the vacuum chamber to react and form a compound on the substrate. Yet another, earlier **METHOD** is referred to as sputtering. In this **METHOD**, a vacuum or gas-filled discharge tube has a cathode that is disintegrated by bombardment, so the cathode material is vaporized and deposited on the substrate.

Linking Sentences from End to Start

The second method of creating cohesion within a paragraph is to place information that is familiar to readers as the subject of the sentence. At the end of the sentence, in the position of emphasis, place new information. In the next

---

EXAMPLE 8

[1] There are no universal guidelines for the level at which glucose intolerance should be labeled as gestational diabetes, making the **DIAGNOSIS OF GESTATIONAL** diabetes controversial (Yogev, Metzger, & Hod, 2009). [2] Currently, for a **DIAGNOSIS OF GESTATIONAL** diabetes, the generally accepted criteria are two abnormal glucose tolerance tests; women identified as having abnormal glucose levels through the screening test then undergo a **DIAGNOSTIC TEST** (Yogev, Metzger, & Hod, 2009). [3] However, **SCREENING** women for gestational diabetes has provoked some disagreement as to how, and if, it should be **SCREENED** for during pregnancy (Yogev, Metzger, & Hod, 2009). [4] **SCREENING** is supported by recent research indicating that higher levels of glucose intolerance lead to poorer pregnancy outcomes and that treatment significantly reduces these **NEGATIVE OUTCOMES** (Hapos et al., 2008). [5] The **EFFECTS OF GESTATIONAL DIABETES** are difficult to determine because of both the varied definitions used in the literature and the different implications of pregnancy, based on if and how gestational diabetes is treated (Yogev, Metzger, & Hod, 2009).

FIGURE 4.8
Linking sentences from end to start.

---

sentence, the new information at the end of the previous sentence becomes the familiar information at the start, and new information is again added at the end of the sentence. This method of cohesion draws on the old information/new information concept of meeting reader expectation.

In Example 8 (see Figure 4.8), the idea in the place of emphasis at the end of sentence 1 ("diagnosis of gestational diabetes," which is set in red typeface) becomes the topic of the succeeding sentence ("for a diagnosis of gestational diabetes"). In sentence 2, the new information about screening women for diabetes then becomes the familiar information at the beginning of sentence 3. The key point to achieving this kind of coherence is that the material in the subject position should link back in some way to what has gone before, and the new information that follows should be located in a place of emphasis, generally at the end of the sentence. You help readers interpret your meaning by articulating its structure, by showing the relationships between your new information and the points that you've previously discussed. Highlighting the links between ideas as you move through the paragraph can increase the chances that your text will be interpreted correctly.

ADDITIONAL READING ON CLARITY AND COHESION

This discussion on clarity is based on George Gopen and Judith Swan's "The Science of Science Writing," *American Scientist* 78 (1990): 550–58. For more information on cohesion and coherence, see Joseph Williams, *Ten Lessons in Clarity and Grace* (Chicago: University of Chicago Press, 2005). A Canadian edition of Williams's book is available: Joseph Williams and Ira Nadel, *Style: Ten Lessons in Clarity and Grace*, Canadian ed. (Toronto: Longman, 2005).

Note: All example texts in this section are used with the permission of the writers.

IN-CLASS EXERCISE 4.6

Create Links between Familiar and New Information

[1] The yield for this experiment was less than expected for several reasons. [2] Initially, before any of the components had been separated, the funnel leaked some of the solution out the stopcock because the rubber ring was disintegrating. [3] This solution was lost into the beaker, and none of it was recovered as product. [4] Further product was not recovered due to a water droplet in the round bottom flask that was used to dry the naphthalene. [5] Because the water was present in the sample, it all had to be redissolved and more drying agent added. [6] Because of the large quantity of drying agent that was in the bottom of the beaker, it was hard to decant all of the liquid out of the bottom. [7] After the first rinse, about half of the drying agent spilled out of the beaker and onto the counter top in the hood. [8] There was some liquid still present with the drying agent when it spilled, which would have contributed to the low yield for naphthalene.

Revising for Plain Language #1

Rewrite the following sentences to make the point clearer and more concise:

1. If the consultant delivers the manual late, the company may cancel the contract.
2. Please leave a voicemail message regarding your absence as soon as possible.
3. Return-on-investment could be calculated for proposed repairs more quickly.
4. This report recommends that the office purchase the new equipment as soon as possible, staff training can begin as soon as the equipment is installed, and every employee should get regular refresher training as new versions of the program come out.
5. Please sign and date the form and send it back to me in the envelope provided at your earliest convenience.

Ten Tips to Make Your Writing Easier to Read

At the word level	1. Use words that are accurate, appropriate, and familiar.
	2. Use technical jargon sparingly; eliminate business jargon altogether.
	3. Use active verbs most of the time.
	4. Use strong verbs (not nouns) to carry the weight of your sentence.
At the sentence level	5. Tighten your writing (eliminate unnecessary words).
	6. Vary sentence length and sentence structure.
	7. Use parallel structure. (See section below on parallelism.)
	8. Put your readers in your sentences.
	9. Begin most paragraphs with topic sentences.
	10. Use transitions to link ideas.

FIGURE 4.9
Ten tips to make your writing easier to read.

CONCISION

Another important element of writing technical prose well is conciseness—using the minimum of words needed to express your ideas, while also remaining clear. Avoid using two words where one word will do. A global initiative, the plain language movement has taken as its focus clarity and conciseness in written language.

Plain Language

Plain language is a movement among business, professional, technical, and government writers that seeks to communicate information to readers as clearly and comprehensibly as possible. This movement has led to a broad revision of health, legal, and government documents in countries such as the UK, Australia, Canada, and the US to ensure that target readers can read and understand the documents that they must use. The plain language movement aims to produce documents that enable readers to "find what they need; understand what they find; and use what they find to meet their needs" (www.plainlanguage.gov/whatisPL/index.cfm). Plain language in the US has a strong government mandate, with President Obama having signed the Plain Writing Act of 2010.

Here are some of the main guidelines published by plain language.gov:

- Find out who your audience is and write for those readers.
- If you have a mixed audience, address each group separately with the information that pertains to it.
- State the purpose of your document first and then the main point.
- Put the central point at the start and only include background information as necessary toward the end.
- Address the reader directly and use "you."
- Use active verbs and the active voice.
- Use the passive voice only when it doesn't matter who is doing the action.

As you can see, plain language focuses on making writing accessible to those who need to read it. Its main principles resemble those already addressed in this chapter, as well as in several other chapters in this book. Figure 4.9 summarizes ten tips at the word and sentence levels that make your writing easier to read.

EXAMPLE 9.1

Arenadeck® has many features that make it a good choice for this project. The most important features are as follows:

- Non-absorbent
- Lightweight
- Extremely durable
- Provides sound and thermal insulation
- Resists contamination
- No warping or deforming
- No flaking, delaminating, or crumbling
- Easy to handle for fast and effective installation and removal
- Non-porous
- Non-sticking to ice
- Easy to clean with just low-pressure washer or floor scrubber
- Covered by a 5-year manufacturer's warranty

EXAMPLE 9.2

Arenadeck is

- Non-absorbent
- Lightweight
- Extremely durable
- Easy to handle for fast and effective installation and removal
- Non-porous
- Non-sticking to ice
- Easy to clean with just a low-pressure washer or floor scrubber
- Covered by a 5-year manufacturer's warranty

Additional useful features include the fact that it

- Provides sound and thermal insulation
- Resists contamination
- Will not warp or deform
- Will not flake, delaminate, or crumble

FIGURE 4.10
Using parallel structures to create coherence.

IN-CLASS EXERCISE 4.8

Revising for Plain Language #2

Revise the paragraph below to make it express the ideas more clearly and plainly. Your readers are students who must work with this policy.

Western University is a community of students, faculty, and support staff involved in learning, teaching, research, and other activities. The University seeks to provide an environment of free and creative inquiry within which critical thinking, humane values, and practical skills are cultivated and sustained. In order to foster and maintain this environment, all members of the University community are responsible for ensuring that their conduct does not jeopardize the good order and proper functioning of the academic and non-academic programs and activities of the University or its faculties, schools, or departments, nor endanger the health, safety, rights, or property of the University or its members or visitors.

Parallelism

Parallelism, the use of matching grammatical structure, is especially challenging in technical and workplace communication when you write lists. Example 9.1 (see Figure 4.10) features a list that starts off all right but then quickly devolves into a confusing series of statements.

The list in Example 9.1 appears parallel initially, but if you add "it is" to the beginning of each item, you quickly encounter entries that don't work: "it is provides sound and thermal insulation; it is resists contamination." The list does not use parallelism because only some list items share related linguistic structures (for example, the first three). The final six items are structured in parallel.

One effective way to revise this list to address the problems with parallelism is to group the similarly structured items together. Some rewording is needed to fit the final items into a parallel structure. (See Example 9.2.)

DEFINING, DESCRIBING, AND EXPLAINING

As a technical communicator, you will frequently adjust your writing to meet the expectations of readers who have varying levels of knowledge of the subject matter. In one document, you might address readers with a sophisticated knowledge of a related field but incomplete knowledge of your subject, for example, health care workers who need to perform a new treatment procedure. This audience requires less background description than a lay or novice audience needs. The health care workers would already know related procedures, so you could build on their existing knowledge. If you are writing primarily for novices, you might define unfamiliar technical terms and generally explain related technical concepts. These scenarios identify two techniques that technical communicators use to produce top quality documents: definition and description.

Definitions are used to explain subject matter related to concepts or terms. If readers are unfamiliar with a term, a well-placed definition can educate them exactly when they need it. A clear definition removes potential confusion and ambiguity. A description is a verbal portrait of something—an object or an event.

Definitions come in three kinds:

- Brief
- Formal or categorical
- Extended

BRIEF DEFINITION

A brief definition is the practice of clarifying the meaning of a word by substituting a more familiar synonym (i.e., a parenthetical definition) or restating a word in different terms to make its meaning clear. For example, in an introduction to Middle Eastern cuisine, the writer uses parenthetical definitions to define clearly and concisely the two terms in the sentence that may be unfamiliar to cooks new to this cuisine: "Tahini (sesame seed paste) is a central ingredient of hummus (chick pea dip), as well as several other popular dishes."

Use a brief definition when your readers do not need detailed information. In the previous example, the parenthetical inserts clarify the potentially unfamiliar terms, and readers who understand the terms without help can ignore these definitions. The following is also a brief definition, although it is longer than the parenthetical versions in the first example:

> The Archimedean screw is a wooden pump that was developed two millennia ago. The screw is encased in a cylinder, and water is lifted up by the screw when the handle is turned. When the water reaches the top of the screw, it pours out into a pitcher or basin placed to catch it.

This definition explains how the Archimedean screw raises water from a river or well to ground level or higher. Two sentences provide you with the main components of the device as well as a brief description of how it works.

FORMAL OR CATEGORICAL DEFINITION

A formal or categorical definition dates back to Aristotle's time in ancient Greece (500 BCE) and consists of three parts:

- The term
- The class
- The features

Table 4.2 lists several examples of categorical definitions (i.e., they "categorize" the term).

Term	Class	Features
LED	Semiconductor	■ Light bulb without a filament ■ Doesn't get hot
Saturated fat	Fats from animals	■ Solid at room temperature ■ Liquid when heated
Artificial Intelligence	A branch of computer science	■ Dealing with the simulation of intelligent behavior in computers

TABLE 4.2
Parts of a formal or categorical definition.
Source for Artificial Intelligence: www.merriam-webster.com.

IN-CLASS EXERCISE 4.9

Writing Categorical Definitions

Choose three technical terms from one of your areas of expertise, and write categorical definitions for each, being sure that the features you use to describe the term differentiate it from other members of the larger class.

The challenge to writing an accurate categorical definition is to use the three parts to specialize the description progressively so that the features listed pertain only to the term being defined. That is, the term lists an unfamiliar concept for readers (artificial intelligence); the class groups the concept into a larger group that shares some characteristics (a branch of computer science); and finally, the features describe the concept further by distinguishing it from the larger group (dealing with the simulation of intelligent behavior in computers). Notice that the definition progresses from the specific term to the more general category to the specific details, so that by the time you describe the features, they should be aspects that apply to the small group only and not to the larger group.

EXTENDED DEFINITION

A third type of definition that you may use is the extended definition, which refers to a more detailed characterization than the previous two. Use them when readers need more detail. The length should be based on both your readers' needs and your purpose in writing it: it may be as short as a paragraph or as long as several pages.

While your choices for creating a brief, parenthetical definition or even a formal, categorical definition are limited, your options for expanding a definition are several. Here is a list of strategies for developing extended definitions and descriptions:

- Operational definition
- Description of parts

- History or background
- Cause and effect
- Analogy or comparison

Operational Definition

An operational definition explains how something works to define what it is. To organize and develop an operational definition, use these three steps:

1. Describe the whole device—that is, give an overview to orient your reader.
2. Explain in detail how the parts work together.
3. Conclude by explaining how the parts work to get the job done.

Figure 4.11 uses this organizational pattern to explain how an atomic clock works. It begins with a brief definition, identifying the two aspects of this clock: how it works and what it's made of. Next it summarizes the clock's components.

The second paragraph identifies the main parts of the clock and explains how they work together. The third paragraph shows how the parts interact to correct one another to measure the one-second interval accurately.

HOW IS AN OPERATIONAL DEFINITION DIFFERENT FROM A SET OF INSTRUCTIONS?

Some students are initially confused about the difference between a set of instructions and an operational definition, especially when they try to define a process operationally. Examine Figure 4.12, and write a paragraph describing how the definition treats the subject matter compared to how the instructions treat it.

IN-CLASS EXERCISE 4.10

Distinguish an Operational Definition from a Set of Instructions

- Which of the two passages in Figure 4.12 is the definition and which is the set of instructions? How can you tell?
- If you tried to make a biscuit joint using only the extended definition, how successful do you think your joint would be? Explain why you think this.

Write down a list of the notable characteristics that distinguish an operational definition from a set of instructions.

FIGURE 4.11
Operational definition of an atomic clock.
Source: Information adapted from howstuffworks.com.

HOW AN ATOMIC CLOCK WORKS

An atomic clock is a precise timekeeper based on measuring the electrical oscillation of an atom, such as cesium 133. An atomic clock keeps time by exciting a series of atoms, passing them through magnetic and microwave fields to alter their energy states, and, from their oscillation frequency, calculating the exact interval of one second.

An atomic clock works by heating cesium in a vacuum tube until the atoms boil. As they boil off, they move down the tube and pass through a magnetic field (the first of two that they will move through). This field collects cesium atoms of the correct energy state, which then pass through a microwave field generated by a crystal oscillator. At some point in each cycle, the microwave field crosses the frequency of 9,192,631,770 Hertz (cycles per second). The cesium atoms change their energy state when they come in contact with this frequency.

A second magnetic field at the far end of the vacuum tube collects those atoms that have changed their energy state. A detector measures the output of changed atoms striking it, and when the output peaks, the peak is used to correct the crystal oscillator and bring the microwave field to the exact frequency. The exact frequency is then divided by 9,192,631,770, which gives one pulse per second, the basic unit of time on our terrestrial clocks.

A. HOW A BISCUIT JOINER WORKS

A biscuit joiner is a small hand-held tool that cuts thin, half-moon-shaped slices of wood from the vertical sides of planed boards so that they can form a strong joint when they are glued together. Think of your tabletop, which is usually fashioned from a series of planks joined side by side. Small, oval wafers of wood coated with glue are then inserted into the half-moon-shaped incisions in the planks and clamped together until the glue dries. A series of skilfully cut biscuit joints will result in a perfectly flat, almost seamless looking tabletop that is both sturdy and beautiful.

B. HOW TO MAKE A BISCUIT JOINT

To make a biscuit joint, you will need the following:

- Two planks of equal thickness
- Waterproof wood glue
- Three or four 5 cm biscuit wafers
- Two or three pipe clamps
- Biscuit joiner

1. Calculate how many joints you will need (space them 8 to 12 inches apart).

2. Mark their locations on the right side of one plank and the left side of the other (i.e., the two surfaces that you will be joining together).

3. Hold the joiner parallel to the edge where you plan to make the joints.

4. Following your placement marks, depress trigger and form first joint.

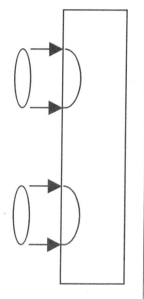

Description of Parts

A third technique for developing an extended definition is to describe the parts of a term or concept. You can use a labeled visual to depict the parts, or you can use a prose description, or both, as illustrated in Figure 4.13. The visual labels the major parts of a sewing machine that are mentioned in the prose description. The prose adds information about how the parts work together. Between the two media, readers gain an understanding of the machine as a whole and how it works.

FIGURE 4.12
An operational definition and a set of instructions.

FIGURE 4.13
This figure uses both a labeled visual and a description to educate readers on the parts of a sewing machine.

A sewing machine consists of several moving and stationary parts. A post on the top holds the spool of thread, while the loose end of the thread is inserted into **THREAD GUIDES** down the front of the machine, through the **PRESSER FOOT** thread guide, to the hole in the needle. On the front side of the machine, you will see three separate sets of knobs: three across the top, one on the left side, and one on the right side. The three knobs at the top (**STITCH CONTROLS**) allow you to select different types of stitches, as well as control the width of the stitches. The knob on the right upright (**STITCH GUIDE**) allows you to control the length of the stitch. The knob on the left side (**THREAD GUIDE**) controls the thread tension, as well as guiding the thread while the machine is running. Under the needle, a series of serrated plates are called the **FEED DOGS**, and they move the fabric under the needle as you sew.

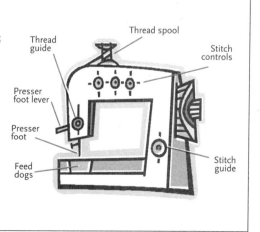

History or Background

A fourth technique for extending a definition is to provide history or background for the term or concept. For example, describe who invented the device or machine and when (if this information is appropriate): "*Nanotechnology* first entered the scientific lexicon back in 1959 in a talk given by Nobel Prize-winning physicist Richard Feynman, when he proposed a new kind of manufacturing that would start with atoms and build up, in contrast to traditional manufacturing which starts with a large quantity of material and cuts away until it creates the finished product."

Another tactic is to elaborate the problem that the device or concept was intended to solve. Figure 4.14 is an extended definition that elaborates the problem that beta-blocker medication was intended to solve.

A third strategy is to highlight key moments through history to show different nuances in the development of the idea or concept. Here is an example:

> The idea of cold fusion has motivated scientific research since the nineteenth century when the ability of palladium to absorb hydrogen was first recognized. In the early twentieth century, several scientists claimed to have fused hydrogen into helium using palladium electrodes. In 1989, two chemists, Stanley Pons and Martin Fleischmann, announced a series of experiments in which they had produced excess heat that appeared to be due to a nuclear reaction. The term "cold fusion," originally invented in 1986 by Paul Palmer for his work with "geo-fusion," was appropriated for the work by Pons and Fleischmann in 1989. (*Source: Information adapted from howstuffworks.com.*)

FIGURE 4.14
This example elaborates one of the medical problems that the medication being defined (beta-blocker) is used to treat.

WHAT ARE BETA-BLOCKER MEDICATIONS?

Beta-blockers are medications used to treat heart disease including atrial fibrillation.

Atrial fibrillation (or congestive heart failure) refers to an irregular heartbeat caused by the disorganized contraction of the heart chambers. In a healthy heart, the chambers contract in a specific pattern. As electrical impulses travel through the chambers, they set off contractions, signaling to the right and left atria to contract. When the atria contract, they pump blood to the ventricles. In the ventricles, the electric impulse stimulates the right ventricle to pump blood to the lungs, while the left ventricle gets a message to pump blood to the rest of the body.

In a person who has atrial fibrillation, this normal rhythm does not happen. Instead the electrical impulses travel randomly through the heart chambers, triggering disorganized contractions that cause a variety of problems and symptoms, resulting in shortness of breath, chest pain, and possibly stroke.

Beta-blockers, used to treat patients with stable atrial fibrillation, work by slowing the heart rate....

Cause and Effect

Another way to describe or define a term or concept is to use cause and effect to explain a process or procedure. For example, Figure 4.15 is part of a longer discussion on groundwater pollution. In defining the factors that contribute to groundwater pollution, the writer elaborates what is meant by "human decisions" by providing an example of how farmers may use pesticides. The decision to apply a pesticide into the soil around plants can lead to the increased likelihood of it leaching through the soil to the groundwater. In addition, deciding to apply the pesticide immediately before irrigating the field or before a downpour is another *cause* that can lead to the pesticide being washed off the field and into drainage ditches (*effect*) and eventually into groundwater supplies.

Groundwater pollution takes place when a number of critical factors are in place. These factors include the type of chemical, the type of soil around the chemical, the proximity of the groundwater at the site, and the decisions of humans at the site. For example, the method used to apply pesticides to a field, as well as the amount used and the timing of the application, can all determine whether the pesticide will reach groundwater reservoirs. If the pesticide is incorporated into the soil, the likelihood that it leaches through the soil will be much higher than if it were applied to foliage or surfaces. Again, if the pesticide is applied immediately before irrigation or a heavy rain, the chances are much higher that it will leach into the soil rather than serve as an effective barrier to crop infestations.

FIGURE 4.15
This example uses both cause and effect (how the pesticide is applied, the likely outcome) and example (human decisions).

Analogy or Comparison

Another effective way to explain a complex concept is to use a comparison or an analogy—that is, to compare the new idea to an ordinary or well-known concept or thing. The areas of similarity between the two entities can help readers understand the key features of the unfamiliar concept and more quickly comprehend it. Figure 4.16 uses an analogy to help readers understand a sophisticated scientific idea, the quantum or potential energy well.

In this case, comparing the quantum well to the furrows of a ploughed field helps readers to imagine the significant features of this type of well and to understand what action is taking place when particles become quantized and tunnel through the barrier.

WHAT IS A POTENTIAL ENERGY WELL?
A potential energy well is a one-dimensional well (imagine the furrows in a ploughed field where the individual furrow extends indefinitely in either direction but is bounded on either side by the adjacent furrows) in which a particle or electron is trapped in the well with infinite boundaries (the length of the furrow) and infinite barriers (the adjacent furrows). The particle (or electron) can move along the plane of the well, but it cannot move through the barrier. After the particle becomes trapped in the well, however, its energy can become "quantized." If the barrier has a finite height and width, then the quantized particle can "tunnel" or move through the barrier, rendering it essentially transparent.

FIGURE 4.16
In this passage, the writer draws an analogy between a potential energy well (in quantum physics) and the furrows in a ploughed field to make clear the significant characteristics of a potential energy well.
Source: Heather Graves, Rhetoric in(to) Science (Cresskill, NJ: Hampton, 2005).

IDENTIFYING METHODS OF DEFINING, DESCRIBING, AND EXPLAINING

Find three or four good examples of extended definitions (howstuffworks.com is a good place to start). Analyze each example to determine which strategies the writer has used to develop the expanded definition or description.

Write a memo reporting the results of your analysis of the three or four examples:

- Which strategies seemed most popular? Useful? (Quote the text critical to your analysis as evidence for your conclusions.)
- Did you identify any strategies that were not mentioned in this section? If so, include them in your report.
- Then write a paragraph explaining which strategies were most popular and why you think they work well in these cases.

DEFINING OR DESCRIBING A TECHNICAL CONCEPT OR DEVICE

Select a technical concept or device and write a definition or description of it using as many of the strategies from this section of Chapter 4 as you can.

- Select a specific audience for your definition/description (not a general audience, but one with a certain level of knowledge of the subject matter).
- Length depends on the complexity of the topic and the needs of your audience.

CHAPTER FIVE

Visual Technical Communication

The graph maker can get away with all kinds of lies simply armed with the knowledge that most readers will not look at the graph very closely.

—Daniel J. Levitin, *A Field Guide to Lies*

USING VISUALS TO COMMUNICATE EFFECTIVELY

Using visuals effectively is an important component of technical communication. Many people who do not understand textual explanations can grasp a complex idea quickly through an effective visual depiction of the same information. Similarly, well and ethically represented information can be highly persuasive. For example, in the early stages of the coronavirus pandemic of 2020, members of the general public were confused about the level of risk the virus posed to themselves and their loved ones. They received conflicting advice through social and news media about the danger the virus posed, and they grew confused about when and then how stringently to begin practicing the social distancing strategies being recommended by medical and government leaders to slow the disease's spread. To help readers understand the situation, the *Washington Post* published a series of images, including animations, that showed how and how quickly a virus could be transmitted among individuals through unrestricted activity (daily life).[1] Other sources such as informationisbeautiful.net created the COVID-19 #Coronavirus Data Pack, a series of graphs that put the risks of this virus in context.[2] Both of these sources provided readers with representations of data that could help them make informed decisions, in the first case, about why to follow advice about social distancing, and in the second case, to remain calm and thoughtful in their responses to the news they received. Good instructional material uses visuals to clarify, communicate, and emphasize.

There is a down side. Poorly designed visuals can also confuse readers and users. If inadequate visuals obscure key information, readers can fail to grasp the implications of a situation. In *Visual Explanations*, graphic artist and researcher Edward Tufte provides examples of ineffective presentations of visual evidence that resulted in disastrous decision-making. He emphasizes that *"there are right ways and wrong ways to show data."*[3] As technical communicators, your challenge is to use visual and verbal information the right way.

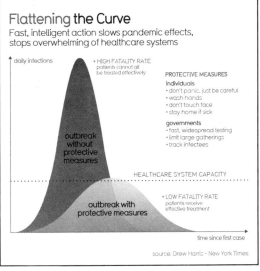

FIGURE 5.1

A visual that effectively illustrates the point of social distancing as a strategy for responding to the spread of COVID-19.

Source: informationisbeautiful.net.

1 Harry Stevens, "Why Outbreaks Like Coronavirus Spread Exponentially, and How to 'Flatten the Curve,'" *The Washington Post*, March 14, 2020.

2 Informationisbeautiful, "COVID-19 #Coronavirus Data Pack," March 16, 2020, www.informationisbeautiful.net.

3 Edward Tufte, *Visual Explanations* (Cheshire, CT: Graphics Press, 1997), 45 (italics in original).

VISUAL COMMUNICATION AND THE WRITING PROCESS

In some academic fields, including chemical engineering, writers are encouraged to begin the writing process by creating visuals before they try to write the text of a report or article. These writers begin by plotting the graphs and preparing the tables that will appear in their reports. These visuals must support the message that they want the report or article to convey. Writing reports that others want to read and giving presentations that audiences find compelling begins with a story: what message do you want to convey to those readers and that audience?

Dan Roam, author of *Back of the Napkin: Solving Problems and Selling Ideas with Pictures,* argues that communicators should be able to use simple visuals to persuade readers and audiences. You should be able to convey the main message from the report you are writing with visuals and a minimum of text: what is the essence of your report? In the text that surrounds your visuals, you will be able to elaborate that essential message by providing details and explanations.

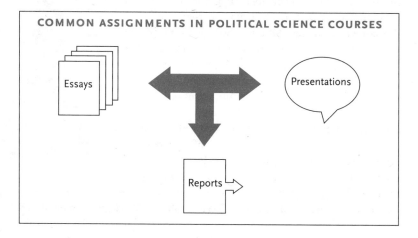

FIGURE 5.1
A concept map shows the links between the three main kinds of ideas; in this case, the visual depicts the assignments that political science undergraduate students are required to write in their courses.

Once you have decided on the story or the message that you want your readers or audience to consider, choose how to communicate that message both in words and visuals. Many readers will begin by skimming and scanning your text rather than reading it from start to finish. To encourage and facilitate these kinds of readers, think about breaking your document into chunks. Use various levels of headings to divide the document into visually distinct units; as a rule, try to limit yourself to three heading levels in shorter reports (fewer than 10 pages). Then refer to your story: what in your report do you want to stress or highlight? Can you make the overall story of your document understandable to readers who skim the headings, look at the visuals, and read the captions?

John Nychka, a chemical engineering professor at the University of Alberta, suggests that writers capture the story that each visual tells by writing a caption for the visual. By writing each caption as a stand-alone chunk of text, writers are forced to state concisely what they want readers to learn from the visual.

WHAT ARE THE "RIGHT WAYS ... TO SHOW DATA"?

The important thing to know about creating visual displays is that each type of chart or graph is better suited for representing a particular type of data. If you have chosen to display a particular type of relationship among your data, you should select the display that will most clearly illustrate that relationship.

For example, a column of numbers will communicate a wealth of information to your readers, but only if they understand how to read the columns and interpret the raw numbers. Many readers are unable or unwilling to do the hard work of comprehending the various meanings embedded in the columns. In addition, there will be more information there than the particular point you intend to make, but there is no guarantee that your readers will divine your exact point from this choice of visual display. As a technical communicator, part of your job is creating a visual that highlights rather than buries the point you want to make to your readers.

How do you decide which type of visual will best display the data that you have selected? First, you need to know what job each type of chart or graph can accomplish. In the section that follows, there is a list of types of visual display, along with a brief summary of what they show most effectively.

SELECT THE RIGHT VISUAL FOR TELLING THAT STORY

Generally, you decide to create a visual when you find an interesting perspective in the data that you have. In other words, you find in the data a **story** that others will find intriguing as well. Never graph numbers just to include a visual: instead, make the visual accomplish a goal. It might undermine common sense ideas about something; it might highlight a new trend or change; it might provide motivation in a persuasive argument. Once you find that compelling story in the data, then you should decide which of the various types of charts will most effectively present these data. Each type of chart is best suited to illustrating a particular relationship between the data, so make sure that you select the method that will best convey your point.

Pie Charts

Use a pie chart to show how a part or parts are related to the whole. Your data do need to be complete (add up to 100 per cent) for a pie chart to make sense.

For example, let's say that you are writing a report for the local Humane Society. You have crunched some of the numbers, and you see that three breeds of dog account for the majority of those given up for adoption last year. You decide to create a visual that will highlight the point that these breeds show up disproportionately at the shelter. Since you know that 187 dogs came into the shelter last year, and you have statistics both on breed and numbers for these dogs, you realize that a pie chart is the best choice to highlight the presence of these dogs.

To emphasize the fact that collies, shepherds, and retrievers account for nearly three-quarters of the breeds brought to the shelter, you decide to emphasize these three breeds using color and representing the other breeds using shades

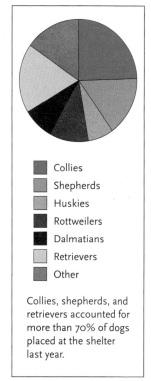

- Collies
- Shepherds
- Huskies
- Rottweilers
- Dalmatians
- Retrievers
- Other

Collies, shepherds, and retrievers accounted for more than 70% of dogs placed at the shelter last year.

FIGURE 5.2
When you have data that add up to 100 per cent, a pie chart can be an effective way to show relationships between the parts and the whole.

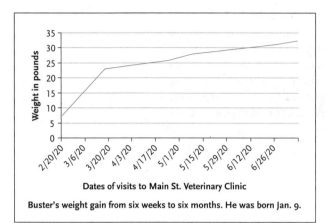

Buster's weight gain from six weeks to six months. He was born Jan. 9.

FIGURE 5.3
A line graph is a good choice to illustrate a growth curve because it depicts the curve clearly and simply.
Source: Main St. Veterinary Clinic medical records.

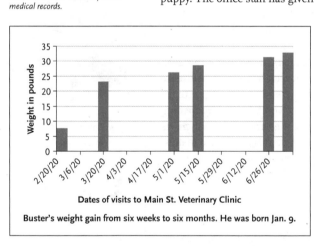

Buster's weight gain from six weeks to six months. He was born Jan. 9.

FIGURE 5.4
The bar chart is a less effective way to illustrate a growth curve because it forces readers to imagine the curve across the top of the bars.
Source: Main St. Veterinary Clinic medical records.

of gray. This format highlights the fact that these breeds disproportionately show up at the shelter, suggesting some kind of issue with these dogs.

The pie chart format allows for comparison of the different groups as well as visually grouping and estimating percentage quantities to make a point clearly and forcefully.

Line Graphs

Use a line graph to compare items over time, to show frequency or distribution, or to show correlations.

For example, you are creating a booklet on puppy care for a local veterinary clinic, a booklet the clinic can distribute to clients as part of its puppy information and care package. Although you have written the informative text for the booklet, you now want to include an effective visual to help readers understand the phenomenal growth curve of a healthy puppy. The office staff has given you some statistics from the clinic's records for Buster, a six-month-old tricolor border collie, that you are using as an example throughout the booklet. You have his weight history at least monthly from the age of six weeks to six months with six measurements in total, so you graph Buster's figures to show his weight gain over that time. You choose a line graph to illustrate his growth curve because you want to compare his change in weight over time.

Bar Charts

Use a bar chart to illustrate comparisons between items, to compare items over time, to show frequency or distribution, and to show correlation.

You could also have used a bar chart to illustrate Buster's growth because a bar chart can also be an effective way to compare items over time. Figure 5.4 shows the same data on Buster's growth presented as a bar chart. While a curve is present along the top of the bars, this presentation requires readers to imagine the growth curve. That makes the bar chart a less clear and effective way of illustrating the comparison in this case.

Dot Charts

Use a dot chart to show correlations.

Dot charts are useful for showing clusters of data so that viewers can see relationships. For example, when you take your Irish wolfhound, Mulligan, to the Main St. Veterinary Clinic, the one for which you created the puppy information booklet, your vet recommends that you protect him from heartworm disease. When you ask about the prevalence of cases in your area, the vet points to a map with all reported cases of the disease marked on it. Figure 5.5 reproduces a dot chart marking cases of heartworm in north-western Washington. Based on the graphic representation of reported cases of heartworm, should you buy heartworm medication for Mulligan?

You see that there is a cluster of cases reported in and around your area of the country, so you decide that it is a wise precaution to protect Mulligan from heartworm.

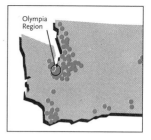

FIGURE 5.5
A dot chart clusters data to show correlation. In this case, if you lived in the Olympia region, you would want to protect your dog from heartworm disease since there were numerous reported cases last year.

Tables

Use tables when the exact figures are important (e.g., measurements to two decimal places).

Figure 5.6 uses a table to present findings from a microbiology experiment. In this case, Kavita Patel selected the table because it was an effective way to summarize the important information and make it easy to check or compare the optimum pH levels for the micro-organisms listed.

Organism	Optimal pH
S. cerevisiae	5.1–6.9
E. coli	8.1 or higher
L. plantarum	3.0 or lower
S. aureus	8.1 or higher

Experimentally Determined Optimal pH of Micro-organisms

FIGURE 5.6
Effective use of a table to enable summary and comparison of findings in a microbiology lab report.

Maps

Use maps to show location or to compare two items. For example, in Figure 5.7, the clip-art image shows the location of the province of British Columbia in relation to the rest of North America.

Photographs

Use photographs to render exact detail or to show something being used. The use of a photograph in Figure 5.8 is effective because it shows the detail of the teeth in the jawbone of this fossil. For extra-large or extra-small objects, include such detail in the photograph to act as a reference point to illustrate the size.

FIGURE 5.7
A map shows the location of British Columbia in relation to the larger context of North America.

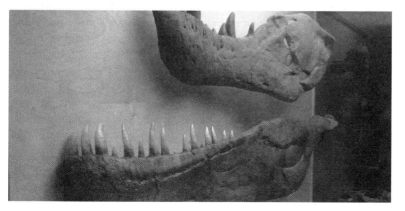

FIGURE 5.8
Display case with fossil specimens at the Royal Tyrrell Museum in Drumheller, AB.

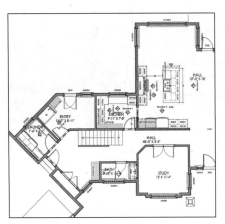

FIGURE 5.9
A line drawing illustrates the room configuration.

Line Drawings

Use a line drawing to emphasize detail or show dimensions.

While photographs are effective illustrations for showing detail, sometimes a line drawing is clearer because it omits distracting detail to focus viewer attention on specific aspects of the item being illustrated. A line drawing reduces the nonessential details and allows viewer focus on the features of the floorplan, including the kitchen layout and how the rooms are configured (see Figure 5.9). While visuals can make details vivid, the *right* visual reduces user confusion and error.

Gantt Charts

Use a Gantt chart to indicate timelines, especially when you are writing a proposal or progress report. If you have created a Gantt chart to outline your schedule in the proposal, then recreate the chart for the progress report, noting the progress of each stage, i.e., which stages are ahead of schedule, behind schedule, or as planned.

USE THE CONVENTIONS FOR TYPICAL VISUALS

A second component to using visuals effectively is following the conventions. Part of the goal in using a visual is to convey a point clearly and efficiently; ignoring or misusing the conventions interferes with readers' or users' ability to interpret the visual quickly and easily.

Re-examine the examples in the section entitled "Select the right visual for telling that story," and try to identify some of the conventions for each type of visual. Here is a list of the conventions that are important:

A Title

The visual should be clearly labeled with a descriptive title that identifies the point you want to convey to your readers.

A Caption

Identify the figure by consecutive numbers in the report. In larger documents, indicate both chapter and figure number (e.g., 5.2 indicating the second figure in chapter 5). Include a caption that directs readers to the story that you are trying to tell by including the figure. Captions range from just a few words to one or two sentences.

All Units Labeled

Both x- and y-axes in graphs should be clearly and legibly labeled, so readers know what the units of measurement are. The items listed in the legend should also be labeled clearly and legibly, and, if you are using color or pattern to identify the items, then the identifying boxes in the legend should be large enough for readers to distinguish one color or pattern from another.

Source of the Data

If you did not create the data yourself, include the source for that information, so users can evaluate its validity or follow up the source if they want to know more.

Source of Visual

If you did not create the visual yourself, also include the source of the visual. If you are using the visual for commercial purposes (rather than for an educational assignment), you may need to request permission to reprint the visual before you publish your document reproducing it. Sometimes, a fee is required for reproduction; sometimes, you need only secure written permission.

VISUALS THAT CONFUSE OR MISLEAD

Sometimes visuals are constructed to mislead viewers deliberately. For example, when an organization is writing its annual report, it might include graphs and charts that obscure the company's poor performance over the past year. Figure 5.10 shows a chart that is designed to present a misleading impression of the statistics it represents. Using increments of 1,000 minimizes the numbers of ill people and deaths in Canada compared to the US, making the virus look minor in Canada. To use smaller increments that better illustrate the lower numbers, the graph should depict a break in the chart to highlight for viewers the fact that space has been omitted in representing the US number of cases.

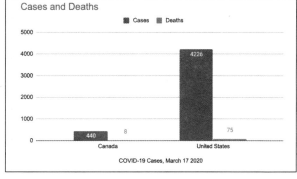

FIGURE 5.10

Using increments of 1,000 captures the large numbers of COVID-19 cases in the US on March 17, 2020 but obscures the numbers of deaths in Canada and minimizes those in the US.

Source: Statistics Canada, March 2020.

Other times, in an attempt to spice up what the writer fears might be a boring visual, he or she may decide to use icons instead of numbers to represent the data being depicted. Figure 5.11 uses icons incorrectly to depict the increasing sales for greeting cards celebrating "Sweetest Day." Edward Tufte calls this use of detail to add visual interest "chartjunk" because it clutters up the clear message that the visual was intended to communicate.

The increasing size of the hearts reflects the increasing sales, but the size of the hearts does not proportionately represent the degree of increase. In addition, the visual does not make clear the fact that sales for 2020 were projected rather than measured. A casual glance at this visual would leave viewers thinking that card sales were exponentially higher in 2020 over 2014, but without clearer reference points, they would have no firm idea of the actual numbers. Note that the units are not represented anywhere, so viewers have no idea whether the sales are measuring hundreds or hundreds of thousands of dollars: as represented, the graph shows only hundreds of dollars, a fact that makes the sales increases unimpressive at best. In this case, a better way to represent the sales would be to use hearts of a uniform size to represent a monetary unit and then reproduce as many hearts as needed to show the actual measured increase. Figure 5.12 uses icons to more accurately represent the figures.

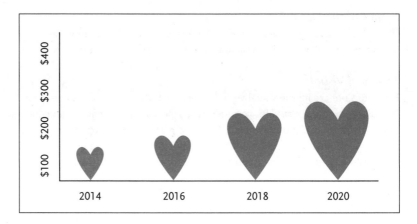

FIGURE 5.11
Sales figures for Sweetest Day are increasing steadily and expected to continue to do so over the next two years; however, this graph does not represent the rate of increase effectively or accurately.

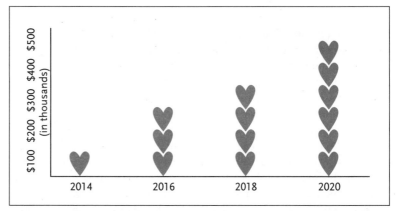

FIGURE 5.12
This icon graph more accurately represents the sales figures, so viewers can judge the increase.

EVALUATING VISUALS

Select a sample of 10 to 15 different types of visuals (preferably choosing at least one example of each type of visual described in this chapter), and analyze each one, evaluating how clear, efficient, and ethical the visual is in presenting the data to the reader.

In a memo report to your instructor, write up your analysis of the visuals, including each sample visual as well as your assessment of it. Make sure that each of your evaluations covers the following topics for each example:

1. the type of visual
2. the completeness of its use of conventions for visuals
3. the "story" that the visual conveys
4. the clarity and ease with which you can identify the point of the visual
5. any improvements you can suggest to the visual to make it clearer or easier to understand.

LAB ASSIGNMENT 5.2

CREATING INTERESTING VISUALS

1. Visit one of these two websites:

- Bureau of Labor Statistics (US government) http://www.bls.gov/oes/home. htm
- Statistics Canada (Canadian government) http://www.statcan.gc.ca

2. Search the site to locate data for the jobs that are projected to be most in demand for the years 2018 to 2024.

3. Create a chart or graph to display this data effectively, highlighting the types of jobs that seem to you to be the most interesting or surprising.

4. Next, identify the job category that you will apply for after graduation, and then identify the wages at the national level, in your home province or state, and in one other province or state.

5. Create a visual that compares these three levels of wages.

6. Research these statistics for three other types of jobs (if you are doing this exercise in groups, then research the jobs of each member of your group).

7. Finally, create a one- to two-page handout that

- reports and synthesizes your findings for question 3,
- synthesizes and reports each group member's answers to questions 4–6, and
- integrates the visuals into your analysis and discussion.

8. Apply everything that you have learned about technical communication so far this term to make this handout as informative and as attractive as possible.

LAB ASSIGNMENT 5.3

EVALUATING THE ETHICS OF VISUAL DISPLAY

Search online for a series of examples of visuals. Alternatively, assemble five to ten printed documents that contain visual display (e.g., annual reports, instructional documents, advertising and marketing materials, etc.) and use this sample for this exercise.

Examine each one in context at the website where you found it (or in context with the other information around it in the print document), and evaluate the effectiveness and the ethical effect of the presentation. Using the information in the previous section of the chapter, evaluate

- whether the visual is the most effective choice for the display,
- whether it presents the data clearly and comprehensibly, and
- whether it displays the data ethically.

Write your analysis in a paragraph or two of text. Make sure your analysis covers the topics mentioned above and draws on the information and vocabulary in this chapter.

CHAPTER SIX

Essentials of Workplace Communication

To help you excel in communications with your co-workers, this chapter introduces you to the essential aspects of workplace writing. Writing in the workplace, like technical communication, often means communicating with overworked readers who may not feel they have time to grant your request. Writing your request to motivate readers to respond is a key focus for workplace writing. Here are some strategies you can use to increase the chances that readers will answer your requests promptly and thoroughly:

1. Know your readers: what are they likely to need or want?
2. Understand what motivates your readers: what are their needs and goals?
3. Organize and present your ideas to show readers how responding to your request can meet their own needs and goals.
4. Build goodwill for yourself and your organization.

To increase the chances that your message is read and acted upon, spend a few minutes analyzing your writing situation before you begin drafting. This analysis should include considering who your readers are, what motivates them to act, and how you might organize and present your ideas to persuade them. The time you spend upfront on planning your message should help you figure out what to say and how to say it. Here are a few topics to help you analyze the situation.

AUDIENCE: WHO ARE YOUR READERS?

If you understand who your readers are, you can better anticipate objections they may have that stop them from granting your request. By identifying possible obstacles, you can adapt your message to remove them in advance, greatly improving the chances of readers responding to your first message.

First, find out who your readers are for a document. The more you know about them, the better you can write the document to show how granting your request can meet their goals too.

Second, determine the demographic characteristics of your readers. Age, gender, economic status, ethnicity, and class also give insight into possible attitudes and beliefs that can affect their response to your message. For more information about analyzing your readers, see also Chapter 1, "Audience, Purpose, Genre, and Medium."

Third, think about how information moves through an organization. What role does your reader play in moving information (formally and informally) through his or her organization? Will communicating with one person ensure everyone knows about your request?

WHAT MOTIVATES YOUR READERS?

Needs can come from outside (extrinsic) or inside (intrinsic). Of the two, intrinsic needs are most powerful because they last. Extrinsic needs can change and are, therefore, potentially not lasting.

Your reader analysis can help you identify needs that readers might have related to your message. Of the motivations you offer, the ones that meet extrinsic needs will be less persuasive than those that meet intrinsic needs, but both types can be effective if your appeal to them is well done.

Figure 6.1 is a mock fundraising letter from the Mid-Atlantic Affiliates of the American Stroke Association that invites readers to make donations. As you read through the letter, note how the appeal targets readers' needs.

The letter targets both basic and higher-level needs of readers. It uses three arguments to show readers how their concerns and interests align with the American Stroke Association's mission to encourage them to donate to its *31 Days of Power* fundraising drive. First, the letter targets readers' basic needs for good health and well-being by pointing out the frequency with which Americans have strokes. Every 40 seconds, on average, suggests a clear and present threat to readers' potential well-being.

Second, the letter comes from the regional branch of the American Stroke Association, the branch in the readers' geographical area. This organization is regional (as opposed to national), and it works "to help you and those you love right here." This emphasis on the regional nature of the foundation highlights the fact that it operates in readers' neighborhoods and makes help available to them and their loved ones. This argument targets the needs of readers to love and be loved; the foundation shares with its readers the need to preserve the health of neighbors and their families.

Third, the letter targets its readers' sense of esteem and desire for recognition. It underscores that any money that this foundation raises will support legitimate research into stroke and heart disease by hospitals and universities in the readers' area. It communicates that a donation to the foundation will contribute to the well-being of society at large. In asking readers to send donations, the writer offers readers the chance to become the kind of people who make possible groundbreaking research to prevent serious illness. In helping others, readers may also end up helping themselves. The letter combines appeals to altruism and self-interest to show readers how their interests are aligned with the fundraising goals of this particular branch of the American Stroke Association.

FIGURE 6.1
Mock fundraising letter
from the American Stroke
Foundation.

American Stroke Association

MID-ATLANTIC AFFILIATES

Dear Friend,

In the next 40 seconds—and every 40 seconds thereafter—an American will have a stroke. Approximately 695,000 strokes occur in America each year! In fact, stroke is the number 4 cause of death in our country.

That is why the American Stroke Association is launching our 20xx *31 Days of Power* fundraising drive in May to help people like you and those you love right here in Maryland, Virginia, North Carolina and South Carolina—and across America. For more than 15 years, the American Stroke Association has worked to build healthier lives, free of cardiovascular diseases and stroke. With our affiliate, the American Heart Association, we have led the way in funding heart and stroke research that has helped to save the lives of millions of Americans. Hundreds of hospital and university-based research teams depend on us to support their efforts to prevent the devastating impact of heart disease and stroke.

But we cannot continue this vital research without your generous support. Please rush your gift of $25, $35, or even $40 or more. And consider joining one of our fundraising events this May. A list of activities in your area is on the Power to End Stroke website (powertoendstroke.org). We depend entirely on friends like you to help those who don't have a minute to spare.

Jane Brown

Jane Brown, Chief Executive Officer
American Stroke Association, Mid-Atlantic Affiliates

ORGANIZE AND PRESENT YOUR IDEAS TO MOTIVATE READERS TO ACT

When you understand your readers' primary motivations, you can then determine how to organize your message, that is, how to order the points that you want to make to show how they align with what will motivate readers. If readers see that helping you also helps them achieve their goals, they will be more likely to grant your request. How do you show readers that helping you will help them meet their goals? Here are several ways to connect your goals with your readers' needs.

Generally:

- Discuss your points in an order that reflects readers' needs.
- Highlight those points that are relevant to readers.
- Use headings and lists to emphasize your main points.
- Anticipate problems or questions and provide solutions or answers.

Specifically:

- Focus on what readers obtain, not on what you are doing for them.
- If you are responding to a request, identify readers' issues specifically.
- Avoid mentioning feelings (yours or theirs).
- Use "you" rather than "I" unless your message is negative.

PURPOSE: GOALS FOR WORKPLACE COMMUNICATION

Good workplace communication, like good technical communication, has both primary and secondary goals (or purposes for writing) in any one document. Obvious goals include making or responding to requests, but four other general goals are often central to each text:

- persuading,
- informing,
- building goodwill for your organization, and
- ending the need for further communication on a topic (as appropriate).

October 30, 20xx

Dear Valued Customer,
Our records indicate that you have not yet submitted your order for October, and we are wondering what the hold-up is. Everyone is busy these days, but you had better take a few minutes to fill out the enclosed order form as soon as possible. If you don't, we will assume that you are choosing the Halloween Special Selection, "Boo! Who? To You," and we will be shipping it to you if we do not receive an alternate order by November 5.

Your membership here at Gift of the Month Club is valued, but for us to do our part we need you to do your part. So please get your order in to us as quickly as you can.

We look forward to hearing from you in a day or two.

Sincerely,
Lisa Gatwick
Sales Associate
Gift of the Month Club
www.giftofthemonthclub.com

IN-CLASS EXERCISE 6.1

Revising to Motivate Readers to Act

The message in Figure 6.2 provides little incentive for readers to comply with the writer's request. Read the message; evaluate which aspects could be improved; and then rewrite the message to better respond to readers' needs.

1. Identify why this message is unmotivating from a reader's perspective.
2. Who is the target audience for this message?
3. Identify two or three goals that readers of this message will have.
4. Rewrite this message to address those goals and to show readers how they will benefit from responding to the request.

FIGURE 6.2
A request that provides readers with little incentive to comply and, indeed, may anger them.

A primary goal for workplace writing can be persuading readers to buy a product or service or to comply with a request. Another goal is to give readers the information needed to understand a new policy or accept a change in procedure. Secondary goals include creating a positive impression of both the writer and the organization that he or she represents. Through these secondary goals, workplace communication also aims to build goodwill with readers. A final secondary goal may be to provide all required information so that readers can respond concerning a topic or understand it fully, making any further communication unnecessary. The message should communicate clearly, concisely, and completely, so writers will not have to request clarification or details.

GENRE: WRITING SHORT MESSAGES (EMAIL, MEMOS, LETTERS)

This section provides the essentials that you need to know about writing the shorter workplace genres: email messages, memos, and letters. Memos are messages sent internally within organizations, while letters are sent to individuals outside of an organization. One exception to this distinction is the email message, which is formatted like a memo but may be sent to people across or outside of organizations.

TIPS FOR WRITING EFFECTIVE EMAIL MESSAGES

Email messages have become the primary means of conveying information in the workplace. In fact, many employees write and receive dozens of electronic messages daily. The prevalence and immediacy of email makes it worth special attention in workplace writing.

KEEP BUSINESS AND PERSONAL EMAIL SEPARATE. You may have a business email account issued by your employer. If you do, **do not use it to send personal email messages**. Employers have legal access to their employees' email accounts, and many can and do screen employee communications. For this reason, do not use your business email to send personal messages or to write comments that you wouldn't want your boss or co-workers to read. In addition, do not read your personal email on a company computer because that may also give the company the right to read those messages.

THINK TWICE BEFORE YOU HIT "SEND." You may receive email messages from co-workers that make you angry or upset. Your first impulse might be to bang out a response to defend yourself or to point out the problem; draft your response in a word processing program, but then throw it away rather than send it. This type of emotional, impulsively sent response generally makes you look unprofessional or petty. Instead, put the message aside for a day or two to consider whether it needs a reply at all. It may not. If it does, think through your response carefully. Avoid emotional language in your response; aim to be professional and neutral in your reply.

IN-CLASS EXERCISE 6.2

Assessing Subject Lines

Evaluate how informative the following subject lines are:

1. Proposal
2. Urgent question about Project 4: Please reply asap
3. About my parental leave
4. Re: Re: Re: Re: Re: May 5
5. New procedures for filing travel claims

Rewrite the poor subject lines, inventing information as necessary to make them clearer and more informative for recipients.

1. Identify and describe the problem.

2. Give whatever background is necessary.

3. Describe options for solving the problem.

4. Recommend a solution and offer assistance to solve the problem.

FIGURE 6.3

How to structure a solution-finding email for your boss.

Writing a Solution-Finding Email to Your Instructor

Let's say you've just discovered that you will have to miss your next technical communication class because you have to attend the funeral of an extended family member, but you have an assignment due at the beginning of that class. Write an email message to your instructor using the information in the previous section and the organizational pattern outlined in Figure 6.3 to help you develop and structure your communication. Remember, you need to both identify and solve the problem that your upcoming absence will create.

PROOFREAD BEFORE YOU SEND. Readers make judgments about you based on the language you use. In workplace email, use standard written English for all of your messages to make your ideas as clear and understandable as possible. Before you send, check the message carefully for words that have letters missing, are misspelled, or that may have been autocorrected to an entirely different word. Look also for grammar or punctuation errors. Don't rely solely on spellcheckers to catch your errors. Read your message aloud to listen for errors in sense or expression.

KEEP PRIVATE INFORMATION CONFIDENTIAL. Government privacy laws protect personal information that some types of businesses use. It is illegal to send email messages outside of your organization's secure intranet if they contain confidential information (for example, social security numbers, birth dates, or credit card information). This information should be stored in locations that are secure from unauthorized viewers. To review these laws, visit the website of the Office of the Privacy Commissioner of Canada (https://www.priv.gc.ca/en/). In the US, a series of overlapping laws cover issues of privacy; individual states including California, New York, and Maryland have created their own comprehensive data privacy laws.

WRITE INFORMATIVE SUBJECT LINES. The difference between a prompt response and silence could be your subject line. Many people receive literally hundreds of emails each week. Most people adopt strategies for dealing with this overload of communication: they evaluate the importance of the message by its subject line. If there is no subject line, recipients skip over the message assuming it is not important. If you need a fast reply, say so; if you are changing the subject of a previous email string, change the subject line.

Writing Emails That Solve Problems

If you hope to have a problem solved through an emailed request, increase your chances by proposing possible solutions to the problem in the message that you send. That way, readers can respond quickly to your email by authorizing you to take the actions you suggest to solve the problem or by scheduling a meeting to discuss the options. If you present a problem without suggesting solutions, readers will set the matter aside until they have time to generate solutions, increasing the likelihood that the problem remains unsolved. Figure 6.3 presents a step-by-step guide.

FORMATTING MEMOS

The conventions for formatting a memo are likely familiar to you from the structure of the header of an email message. Figure 6.4 indicates the key features of memo format. Memos are generally 1 to 1½ pages long, and they communicate information among readers within an organization. To communicate information to readers outside your organization, use a business letter.

MEMO .

To: [put your reader's name here]

From: [put your name here]

Date: [put today's date here]

Subject: [write a brief statement of the memo's subject here]

Then start writing your memo here. If headings are appropriate, use them in the body of your memo to signpost important topics related to your subject and to help your reader understand your message.

FIGURE 6.4
Conventions for formatting a memo.

Your name
Address
Phone number
Today's date

Recipient's name
Company name
Address

Subject: [What the letter is about]

Dear [Recipient's name]:

Leave a two to three cm or one inch margin on all sides of the letter. If you are using letterhead, omit your name and address information. Just start with today's date, the recipient's name, and the company's name and address.

Left align all parts of the letter. Leave a space between paragraphs, and do not indent the first line of paragraphs.

Sincerely,

[Your signature]
Your name
Your title

Enclosures: [Number of enclosures]
Cc: [Names of people copied]

FIGURE 6.5
Conventions for formatting a business letter using block format.

FORMATTING BUSINESS LETTERS

The simplest way to format a business letter is to use a block format. This means that all parts of the letter are aligned along the left margin and you leave a space between paragraphs but do not indent them. Figure 6.5 outlines the conventions for formatting a business letter. As mentioned, leave a two to three cm or one inch margin around all four sides of the page. If you are using letterhead, omit your address information.

WRITING MESSAGES

IN-CLASS EXERCISE 6.4

Revising a Positive and Informative Message

Using the sample message in Figure 6.8, analyze the structure of the letter:

1. Identify which elements of Jenna Smith's response correspond with the pattern of organization outlined in Figure 6.7.
2. Evaluate the quality of Smith's response, and note areas of the message that you think could be improved.
3. Revise the message to Ms. Graves to improve the areas that you noted.
4. Submit a copy of your analysis and revision to your instructor.

The messages that you write in the workplace will fall into four general categories:

- informative,
- positive,
- negative, and
- persuasive.

These categories refer to the main purpose and tone of the message: how might readers respond to the information you communicate? Decide which kind of message you should write based on your expected response from readers. For example, if you expect readers to feel neutral toward the information that you write, the message is informative. If readers should feel happy about the message you are sending, it is positive. In contrast, if you think readers may be upset or angry at your message, it is negative. And if you expect readers to resist or oppose your message, it should be persuasive.

INFORMATIVE MESSAGES

Informative messages usually present readers with information they need (or you need them to have); they also encourage recipients to read, understand, and respond, either neutrally or positively, to this information; and, finally, they downplay any negative elements.

Figure 6.6 outlines a basic structure that you can use to organize an informative message. Note how this pattern also incorporates reader motivation to encourage readers' positive responses.

POSITIVE MESSAGES

Positive messages have several goals including: sharing good news; downplaying any negative elements; and ensuring that readers read, understand, and respond positively. As you will see by comparing Figures 6.7 and 6.8, the pattern for organizing positive messages is similar to that for arranging informative messages.

---

1. Present main points briefly.
2. Add details and include all relevant information.
3. State any negative elements as positively as you can.
4. Include additional details to highlight how readers benefit from this information.
5. End with a goodwill closing.

FIGURE 6.6
A basic organizational pattern for an informative message.

---

1. Briefly present the main points and share any good news.
2. Add details and include all relevant information that readers need.
3. State any negative elements as positively as possible.
4. Show readers how this message benefits them.
5. Close with a goodwill ending.

FIGURE 6.7
A basic organizational pattern for positive messages.

Figure 6.8 presents an example of a message that is both positive and informative. It uses the pattern outlined in Figure 6.7.

To: hgraves@yahoo.com
From: jesmith@elitemachines.com
Subject: Washing Machine User Manual
Date: January 7, 20xx

Dear Ms. Graves,
Thank you for your recent message inquiring about how to obtain a user
manual for your new washing machine. Elite Machines stopped shipping user
manuals with our new appliances several years ago to adopt greener business
practices. Instead, we post online versions of our appliance user manuals
on the company's customer service page. This policy allows us to revise our
user manuals regularly to ensure customers have access to the most up-to-
date information whenever they need it. It also allows customers to access the
correct manual whenever convenient for them.

Here is the webpage where you can find a copy of the manual for your model:

www.elitemachines/customerservice/appliances/wash.html

Please note that the online manual has a clickable table of contents where you
can jump to the specific section that you need. If you desire to download the
manual, you may do so; however, please remember that the online version will
always contain the most current information.

If you have difficulty locating the manual for your appliance model, please use
Elite Machines' help service (www.elitemachines/customerservice/help.html) to
ask questions about any of our products and receive a timely response from one
of our online help staff.

Again, thank you for purchasing an Elite Machine for your washing needs.

Sincerely,
Jenna E. Smith
Customer Service Representative
Elite Machines Inc.
www.elitemachines.com

FIGURE 6.8
A positive and informative
message that uses a traditional
pattern of organization.

NEGATIVE MESSAGES

Negative messages are those that you expect readers to receive with anger or
disappointment. The goal of a negative message is to communicate the information in a way that readers can accept, to diffuse any negative emotions as
far as possible, to forestall any additional communication on this topic, and to
maintain the reader's goodwill toward the writer (you and your organization).

You can organize a negative message in two ways, either with a buffer or
without (see Figure 6.9).

Using a Buffer

A buffer is a neutral or positive statement that delays the negative information
but does not signal it. After this buffer, the negative information is stated once

clearly (but not repeated). If you can offer readers alternatives or a compromise about the negative circumstances outlined by the information, these choices are then described briefly. Ensure that you include any details that readers will need to act on the alternatives or compromises that you offer (to forestall additional communication, if possible). Close with a positive ending that builds goodwill.

Writing a Good Buffer

Ideas for writing good buffers include using any positive information that you have to begin. Other good buffers:

- thank readers for something that they've done (i.e., sending you an order),
- summarize events or facts related to the situation, or
- refer to an enclosure sent with the message.

A good buffer puts readers in a positive frame of mind without suggesting that positive information follows, and it transitions effectively to the negative information.

Alternative to a Buffer

If you choose not to use a buffer, begin your message by stating the reason for the negative information or refusal, followed by the negative information itself (stated once, clearly). The rest of the message is organized following the pattern outlined when you use a buffer.

BEGIN WITH A BUFFER
1. Open with a buffer (a neutral or positive statement to delay the negative).
2. State the negative information once clearly.
3. Present any possible alternatives or compromises.
4. Close with a positive, goodwill ending.

BEGIN WITH THE REASON
1. State the reason for the negative information or refusal first.
2. State the negative information once clearly.
3. Present any possible alternatives or compromises.
4. Close with a positive, goodwill ending.

FIGURE 6.9
Two patterns of organizing negative messages.

To: jon.black@blackhome.shaw.ca
From: jschwartz@blencairngaming&technicalsupport.com
Date: April 17, 20xx
Subject: DigiPro 20xx Expansion Pack Availability

Because we no longer stock AllPro Game Engine software, we are unable to make the new DigiPro 20xx expansion pack available to you. However, there are several online gaming sites that continue to handle AllPro Game Engine software where you should be able to obtain a copy of the expansion pack. These sites include Calling All Gamers, Megamode Download, and Fear the Reaper. The URLs for these websites are easily obtained through an online search engine such as yahoo! or google.com. We apologize for any inconvenience, and we hope that you enjoy your expansion pack once you find a copy.

Jason S.

FIGURE 6.10
A sample negative message that gives the reason first.

PERSUASIVE MESSAGES

Persuasive messages are those that you expect readers to resist. For example, your organization might change reimbursement procedures for employee travel, requiring you to submit boarding passes along with your ticket receipt so that your refund comes several weeks following your return. Employees will likely be displeased and resistant because this change means that they have to fund the trip personally until after they return. The challenge of writing the memo to inform everyone of this new policy requires convincing readers to follow this new procedure and to understand and accept that it is necessary.

Persuasive messages fall into two categories: direct requests and solution-finding messages. Direct request messages ask readers to do something; solution-finding messages identify a problem and propose a solution.

Direct Request Messages

When you ask readers to do something for you, you are asking them to act. People act when they are motivated to do so. Motivating readers requires that you know how or what they think, for example, anticipating resistance they might have to your request. To figure out possible sources of resistance or objections, ask readers (if they are available) or analyze them and the situation to identify potential obstacles.

Obstacles or objections often arise from three areas:

- emotional reasons,
- practical reasons, or
- misapprehension.

Consider the example of the new travel reimbursement procedures: readers might resist because they feel the new system indicates that the company no longer trusts them to take a flight after they book it. They have to provide "proof" in the form of boarding passes that they actually took the trip. These readers would have to be convinced that the change—requiring boarding passes—does not reveal an untrusting attitude by their bosses. Other readers may object to the new policy on the practical grounds that they do not have enough savings to advance trip costs up front and wait for later reimbursement. Arguments would have to be developed to show these readers how the policy change actually benefits them.

HOW TO ORGANIZE A DIRECT REQUEST

Figure 6.11 outlines a pattern for structuring a direct request. Use this basic pattern as a starting point for drafting this type of message, and alter it as needed to fit your specific situation. For example, if you are writing to your boss, who is already acquainted with the details, you might omit the background summary of the subject.

IN-CLASS EXERCISE 6.6

Overcoming Obstacles to Reader Acceptance

Use the example of a company policy change that requires all employees to submit boarding passes with airline receipts before they can be reimbursed for business flights. In groups of two or three,

1. Brainstorm a list of possible objections that various readers (e.g., your boss, student interns, or co-workers) might have to the new policy.
2. Generate a list of arguments to use in the memo announcing this policy change that might overcome the objections identified in #1.
3. Draft a paragraph or two that announces the policy change and that uses some of the arguments created in #2 to anticipate and overcome potential reader objections to the new policy.
4. Hand in your draft at the end of class.

---

1. Introduce the subject.
2. Summarize the background to the subject (postpones request to avoid being rude or too direct).
3. Request action.
4. Include all details so the reader can act.
5. Motivate the reader to act on the request.
6. Remove obstacles to reader action and acceptance.

FIGURE 6.11
Basic organizational structure for a direct-request message.

IN-CLASS EXERCISE 6.7

Writing a Direct Request Message

Assume you are an intern at a software engineering firm, and you have just received an email about a software engineering conference that you would like to attend. Using the basic organizational structure outlined for a direct request message in Figure 6.11, draft an email to your supervisor inquiring about the possibility of attending this conference as part of your work experience. Make sure to explain why this experience will benefit him or her as well as you.

Solution-Finding Messages

A solution-finding message generally identifies a problem (shared by you and readers) and proposes a solution. This type of message becomes persuasive when you induce readers to accept (and act on) the solution that you propose. As in direct request messages, consider whether readers might object to your solution so that you can anticipate and overcome any potential obstacles.

HOW TO ORGANIZE A SOLUTION-FINDING MESSAGE

Figure 6.12 outlines a basic pattern for structuring a solution-finding message. Again, use it as a starting point for your message, and adapt it to fit your situation.

. Review the message in Figure 6.13; you will see it uses the basic structure for a solution-finding message.

1. Begin by making a connection with your reader that shows you are on the same side when it comes to finding a solution to the problem.
2. Then describe the nature of the problem, highlighting how both you and the reader need a solution.
3. Next describe the key features of your proposed solution.
4. Generally, you need some kind of action from your reader (for example, permission to implement the solution that you propose), so explain clearly what you want him or her to do and why it matters.
5. Finally, explain how your solution will benefit your reader.

In the example in Figure 6.13, the writer ends by noting that the proposed solutions will result in the benefit they both want: a successful trade show experience for all of their employees.

FIGURE 6.12
Basic structure for organizing a solution-finding message.

> 1. Establish common ground with your readers.
> 2. Describe the shared problem.
> 3. Explain the proposed solution.
> 4. Explain why the action requested is necessary.
> 5. Show how readers benefit from this solution.

To: Eileen Starke
From: Rob Brown
Date: Sept. 22, 20xx
Subject: Tech Expo & Trade Show in Las Vegas

You were absolutely correct: we are almost too late booking our trip to the Tech Expo & Trade Show in Las Vegas in November. The main hotels recommended by the organizing team are all booked, and most of the highly rated restaurants are fully booked as well, meaning we have to develop a plan B for our awards night.

Here is what I propose for Problem One: I was able to put a 24-hour hold on a block of rooms at the Marriott Suites (pending your approval), which is closer to the airport and about seven miles from the trade show. Seven miles is too far for most of the team to walk, and the public transportation in LV is unpredictable, so we would have to arrange transportation for most of the team. However, I looked into renting two vans (each seat 8 plus the driver), and with the cheaper cost of rooms at the Marriott (over the trade-show hotel), these accommodations and transportation arrangements are still within budget.

For Problem Two: Maureen (from Accounting) grew up in LV, and she recommends a restaurant, Nopale Junction, which is four blocks from the trade-show hotel and which still has a room about the right size for our banquet. I checked out online reviews, and NJ has some good ones from locals. It offers tex-mex fusion cooking with some food allergy options, which will fit our team quite well. Given the scarcity of options and the recommendation for this place by one of our employees, I suggest we reserve the NJ banquet hall for our function.

Please let me know what you think about these solutions. I can look further for a banquet room, but we will have to make a decision in the next day or two because the hold comes off of these arrangements on Friday at 5 PM. As soon as you give me the go-ahead, I can make some reservations, and we will have most of the amenities in place that we will need for a successful trade-show experience.

FIGURE 6.13
A solution-finding message based on the outline in Figure 6.12.

CHAPTER SEVEN

Progress Reports, White Papers, and Recommendation Reports

Generally, reports are characterized by two qualities: they contain a "systematic record of a particular technical study" and they are usually written for others to read.[1] Reporting technical information means keeping in mind the needs of your readers who *may* but likely *do not* share the same level of knowledge of specialized subject matter that you do.

To help both kinds of readers make their way through your documents, design them to enable readers to skim and scan. Use white space, headings, and lists to make it easier for readers to jump around and from section to section. Headings help them scan the document and then skim over text they are already familiar with. Other techniques include defining technical terms or concepts to help readers navigate through your discussion. These definitions can be parenthetical (presented in parentheses in the sentences of the main body of your text, as this definition is), or they can be given in footnotes, in call-out boxes, or in a glossary or appendix. See Chapter 4, "Writing Technical Prose," for more information about defining technical terms and concepts.

This chapter focuses on four different types of reports:

- the status or progress report
- the information report or white paper
- the laboratory report
- the recommendation report

You will find information about what you are trying to accomplish in writing these reports, how to format the different genres, and useful strategies for responding effectively to the rhetorical challenges presented by these types of reports.

1 Hans F. Ebel, Claus Bliefert, and William E. Russey, *The Art of Scientific Writing: From Student Reports to Professional Publications in Chemistry and Related Fields*, 2nd ed. (Weinheim, Germany: Wiley-VCH, 2004), 7.

STATUS OR PROGRESS REPORTS

Status reports are also known as progress or activity reports, depending upon the focus of the report. Activity reports are generally used as a way for employees to update supervisors on how they have spent their workweek, noting accomplishments on various assigned tasks or alerting managers to potential or real problems that may be looming. Status or progress reports generally focus on the progress of a particular project. In some organizations, all three terms may be used interchangeably to refer to the same type of document.

PURPOSE OF STATUS REPORTS

Writing a status report fulfills several functions in an organization:

- to update team members and managers on the progress and status of projects within an organization,
- to show an organization's or individual's competence in pursuing and completing a task, and
- to help those doing the work to assess it and plan future work.

Status reports document the progress of work at an organization. They provide concise, coherent, and clear summaries of what work has been completed and what work remains. Many organizations have employees write one-page status reports each week to account for how they have spent their time. Supervisors scan these reports to ensure that employees are productively engaged and projects are moving ahead.

STRUCTURE OF A STATUS REPORT

Beginning:

Introduction or project description

This section should refresh your reader's memory on your project and briefly summarize its central points.

Middle:

Work completed

- Task 1
- Task 2

This section details the work that you have completed, task by task. If you encountered any problems with these tasks, you also describe the actions that you took to resolve the difficulties.

Work remaining

- Task 3
- Task 4

This section describes the tasks that still remain before you complete the project. It lists the tasks that remain, but with limited elaboration. Mention any potential obstacles that you anticipate and propose solutions.

Cost

Report on how much of the budget has been used to this point and how much remains. Explain any discrepancies between the plan and reality.

End:

Overall assessment of progress to date, conclusions and recommendations

Conclude by appraising your progress for your supervisor. Assess whether the project will be completed as anticipated in the proposal. If you have any recommendations about changes to the plan or schedule, include those here.

FIGURE 7.1
A generic structure for a status report. Adapt this structure to your rhetorical situation.

Status reports also perform a rhetorical function by giving writers the opportunity to demonstrate either their own or their company's competence and ability. For example, if you reach the goals set out in the original project proposal each week, you can highlight this fact in the status report. If you encounter an obstacle to reaching the goal but also develop a solution that quickly gets the project back on track, you can emphasize your successful problem-solving abilities in the status report.

CONTENT OF STATUS REPORTS

Usually the status report contains information about the status of all current projects:

- It summarizes what has been accomplished.
- It supplies information about any problems.
- It describes the actions taken to resolve problems.
- It outlines the writer's plans for the coming weeks.

Figure 7.1 lists a generic outline for a status report. If your organization doesn't have its own format, then adapt it to your situation.

WRITING THE STATUS REPORT: RHETORICAL CONSIDERATIONS

A status report is both an informative and a persuasive document. You should have two persuasive goals: describing the ongoing progress toward your project's success and demonstrating your competence and ability as an employee.

Since the status report is a persuasive document, assess what you are writing and how you are writing it. Present the information on your progress as clearly and accurately as you can. Provide the level of detail necessary to convey your progress unambiguously, but also recognize that your reader has many other responsibilities. If in doubt, move long descriptions to an appendix and let your readers decide if they want to read that material.

You also want to demonstrate your competence. Include details that show your commitment and expertise. If you are going to make generalizations about your progress, support them with detailed factual accomplishments. If you have encountered problems that have slowed your progress, present those problems honestly, and, if possible, emphasize positive solutions. For example, if the web design team has learned that the original layout needs revision based on user feedback (i.e., test users could not find the navigation bar), explain which changes the team thinks will make the navigation bar more prominent, and note that additional informal testing suggests that this revision eliminates the problem without introducing new ones.

Do not skip over problems that have delayed progress. It will *not* be easier to break the bad news later that the project will miss its deadline. Supervisors appreciate knowing early that the project is behind schedule. If they are not informed promptly about delays, they will assume that everything is going well—until the product is not ready for its release.

Figures 7.2 and 7.3 are examples of a student-written status report prepared for Major Project 7.1. In this memo, Rebecca McGregor reports on the progress of her proposal to create a training manual for computer engineering students who arrive for a work term at ArenaSystems Inc., a company that manufactures dasher boards for hockey and indoor soccer arenas.

MEMO

To: Professor Chang
From: Rebecca McGregor
Subject: Status report on training manual for co-op students at ArenaSystems Inc.
Date: October 7, 20xx

Project Description

ArenaSystems Inc. is a growing manufacturing firm that produces arena boards for inline skating pads, hockey rinks, and indoor soccer fields. Recently, they have hired several mechatronics engineering co-op students to help write programming code for a robot they have installed that will increase productivity as well as product quality. So far, the company lacks orientation or training information to help new co-op students quickly learn the basics about the business. I am writing a manual that documents the basic information and procedures that new students need to know about ArenaSystems Inc. This manual will be a quick reference to answer basic questions that students may have about the products that the company sells and the procedures that they need to know as they get started on their assigned projects. The manual covers the following topics:

- Overview of ArenaSystems' products and specialties
- Brief description of key employees and their areas of expertise and responsibility
- Previously undocumented office procedures often assigned to co-op students (e.g., how to answer the phone and direct calls).

Work Completed
Interviews conducted: content selected
This project is progressing well. I have hit my deadlines to this point, having selected the content for the manual and drafted the first five pages, which give an overview of the company and its products. I had a bit of trouble scheduling the interviews at first because two of the three people I needed to talk to were out of town during the week that I had scheduled to interview them. However, I was able to meet with them early the following week, and they were very helpful in suggesting what information they wanted new employees to learn. I drafted an outline of the content and had it approved on September 30.

FIGURE 7.2
Sample status or progress report (page one).

LAB ASSIGNMENT 7.1

WRITING A STATUS REPORT

Using the information in this section, write a status or progress report on your degree progress for either your parents or your undergraduate program academic adviser. Accurately report the work that you have completed thus far, and also explain the work that still remains. Remember to report your progress as positively as possible, but don't minimize problems that you've encountered.

R. McGregor—2

Work Remaining

After deciding on the manual content and drafting the first third, covering ArenaSystems' products and specialties, I only have to write the personnel and responsibility descriptions and to document the office procedures that I had to learn during the first few weeks of my work term. To illustrate these procedures, I will use a combination of digital photos and screen shots. The owners have given me permission to visit the company this weekend to create the visuals, and I am hoping that I can complete the draft and the graphics by Oct. 17.

Midterms start on Oct. 18, and that may slow down my progress on the usability testing. However, I have built extra time into my project schedule, so I expect to complete the tests on time, even if studying for midterm exams delays my actually running the tests. Two employees of ArenaSystems have agreed to help me test the manual, and my roommate is going to serve as the third test user.

Overall Progress

There has been no major delay to this project. I still have two-thirds of the work to do to complete the draft, but the original schedule seems reasonable, if I continue to complete the tasks as listed. Since I have already lined up my test users and tentative dates for testing, I expect that this project will be completed, tested, and revised by the deadline for this project, December 3.

FIGURE 7.3
Sample status or progress report (page two).

MAJOR PROJECT 7.1

REPORTING PROGRESS ON YOUR DEGREE

Write a relatively short (one to two pages) status report on your degree progress. Address the memo to a potential summer employer, and organize your discussion around the points below (taken from this section of the chapter).

Status Report Content

Summarize your progress in terms of your goals and your original schedule.

- Use measurable statements.

Work Completed

- Describe which requirements have been fulfilled already.
- Be specific to support your claims in the first paragraph and so your reader can appreciate your hard work.
- Acknowledge the people who have helped you.
- Describe any serious obstacles that you've encountered, and explain how you've dealt with them.

Work to Be Completed

- Describe the coursework that remains.
- Discuss your plans after graduation.

Overall Assessment of Progress

- Express your confidence in graduating on time, or
- If you are behind in your original schedule, explain how your secondary timetable is workable.

WHITE PAPERS OR INFORMATION REPORTS

White papers (information reports) are reports that provide information about a topic. Originally white papers were government reports that presented authoritative and reputable information about that topic. Businesses and industry have adopted the genre as a way of informing readers outside their organizations about services and products they offer. Generally white papers perform two types of rhetorical activities: 1) they propose a solution to a problem, or 2) they advocate a position on the topic. The FIRST KIND of white paper are often MARKETING tools that discuss innovations in technology or new products; writers frame their product or service as a solution that meets readers' needs. In technical fields, especially in the information technology industry, white papers are both technical documents and marketing documents. From a company's perspective, their purpose is generally threefold:

- to inform readers,
- to educate them about the advantages of a new product or service, and
- to persuade them that this innovation is the superior solution to a particular problem.

These goals make this type of white paper both an informative and persuasive genre of technical communication. From the reader's perspective, this type provides useful sources of information about innovative products and services: busy executives review them to find solutions to problems and to justify the solutions they choose. In fact, more than three-quarters of information technology professionals review white papers on a topic before they make a purchasing decision.

The SECOND KIND of white paper, ones that argue a POSITION, are generally informational as well as persuasive. They may identify problems that have arisen with technological innovations, argue for further advancement in particular research directions, or they may explore the implications of problems or lack of innovation and discuss possible solutions to those problems.

As both technical and marketing documents, white papers present unique challenges for writers. They often present complex technical information to a broad audience of readers. Given the non-specialist character of your audience, you should avoid using technical jargon or acronyms that can make readers impatient. On the other hand, you can also run the risk of being too promotional in a white paper, selling the product or service too hard, which also turns readers off. Your goal in writing a white paper, then, is to strike a balance between informing and persuading your reader.

WHAT INFORMATION DO YOU PUT IN A WHITE PAPER?

The most effective approach to organizing a marketing white paper is to begin by describing a common problem or scenario that both grabs readers' attention

---

FORMAT FOR A TECHNICAL WHITE PAPER

Total length: 5 to 50 pages (optimum length found to be 15 to 20 pages)

Abstract or Executive Summary
length: One paragraph
content:

- Summarize the purpose of the paper
- Summarize your findings
- Some controversy over whether to include conclusions in your abstract:
  - Not including the conclusions entices the reader to look beyond the abstract.
  - Including the conclusions results in busy executives not reading further.

Problem Statement
length: Two to three paragraphs
content:

- Describe the problem
- Give a brief background or context for the problem:
  - Avoid technical jargon.
  - Define essential technical terms.

Description of Solution
length: As long as needed, as short as possible

- Describe what you propose as a solution (how product or service works in general [informing goal], actions reader can take to mitigate the problem)
- Enumerate the features of the solution (product or service, steps to take)
- Explain how product, service, or your suggested actions apply to the problem stated above
- Include visuals that illustrate the product or explain the service

How Product/Service/Your Proposed Solutions Solve the Problem
length: As long as needed, as short as possible

- Show how the product, service, or your proposed solutions apply to the problem (persuasive goal)
- Include evidence
- Show how features of product/service/suggested actions benefit the reader
- Explain why what you propose is superior to other possible solutions
- Acknowledge one or two limitations to demonstrate an unbiased assessment of the solution

Conclusion
length: One or two paragraphs

- Summarize why your product, service, or suggested action is the best solution to the problem

---

FIGURE 7.4
Format for an effective white paper.

and illustrates that you understand the problem confronting them that they need to solve. After describing the problem, you explain the solution and introduce the new product or service. Next, show how it helps to solve the problem. Finally, you conclude by emphasizing why it is the best solution.

To organize a position white paper, you could begin in a similar way by describing a scenario, but your goal might be to prompt readers to think in new ways about the innovation. You might review the features of the various products and evaluate them, but then discuss some of the broader social implications of these examples (see, for example, Katrice Blackwell's research on augmented (AR) or extended reality (XR) in Figures 7.7 and 7.8). Instead of presenting one product or service as a solution in the position white paper, you might summarize strategies that readers should consider to mitigate the problem for how they choose to use the new technology.

Writing a good white paper means solving some rhetorical challenges. Primarily, you are making an argument: for example, to demonstrate that the new product or service is the best solution to the problem you have identified, or that the risks you identify are valid and worthy of wider attention. Figure 7.4 outlines the format for an effective white paper, and Figures 7.5 and 7.6 excerpt sections from a sample marketing white paper, following this format, written by Lisa Richards on a new product called "Web-Time," an online service that allows temporary employees (temps) to submit their hours through the Internet rather than by filling out paper timesheets. Figure 7.5 reproduces the executive summary and first part of the problem statement. In Figure 7.6, the solution to the problem is reproduced. Note that Richards also includes a visual (one of three) that illustrates and supports the solution she describes.

FIGURE 7.5
Executive summary and first part of problem statement from a white paper by Lisa Richards on an online service that allows temporary employees to submit their timesheets over the Internet.

Executive Summary

This report evaluates the existing methods for employees to submit the hours that they have worked to their respective temp agency. Currently, many temp agencies use a paper-based method that encourages waste, inefficiency, and can reduce company productivity.

A new service called "Web-Time" gives employees a valuable alternative to filling out paper timesheets by submitting them online instead. Throughout this report, the costs and benefits of using Web-Time as opposed to paper timesheets will be compared and contrasted. Web-Time has proven itself to be the most useful and effective method of submitting time cards, and the reasons for its successes will be evaluated and explained in further detail.

Problem Statement

Technological advancements have created more efficient ways to cope with situations that we face in our daily life. These new methods of doing things are not only more efficient, but can be environmentally sound and financially profitable. Businesses are embracing these technologies by shifting from paper-based systems to electronic processes. Examples include online banking, online course registration at universities, and email. These systems have proven themselves to be invaluable as they save time, frustration, and (occasionally) money for the people who use them.

In the past, employees used to have to punch time cards to mark the beginnings and endings of their shifts as a means of logging their hours. Punched time cards became outdated, and society advanced to filling in timesheets that could be mailed (or even better, faxed!) to employers. Once again, old methodology has become obsolete and has been replaced by a new process.

At First Data Merchant Services, most of the employees have been contracted by assorted temp agencies; they all have different schedules and work in various departments of the business. To keep track of the number of hours worked, each week, employees must fill in timesheets that detail what specific hours they worked between, how long their breaks were, and what days they worked.

HOW WEB-TIME SOLVES THE AFOREMENTIONED PROBLEM

Web-Time allows employees to log their hours online and then submit the hours to their respective supervisors. Each supervisor is then able to log in at his/her own convenience, verify the hours of the employee, and then submit them directly to the temp agency online. (See Figure 3.) The goal of Web-Time is to reduce the amount of time that is wasted by both employees and supervisors and to make it more convenient to submit/verify hours at one's own leisure.

Web-Time is a cost-effective solution for both the temp agency and the company (in this case, First Data) because it reduces printing costs of timesheets and the individual sheets of paper wasted from the fax machine. This system alleviates the stresses of manually filling in a timesheet, rechecking the hourly figures to ensure accuracy, finding a supervisor for a signature, faxing the timesheet, and then waiting for a confirmation to ensure that it was received by the temp agency. Since employees will be able to complete and submit their hours quickly online, they will be able to concentrate on doing their job efficiently and to the best of their ability, which can lead to increased performance and productivity.

Figure 3: Completed Timesheet

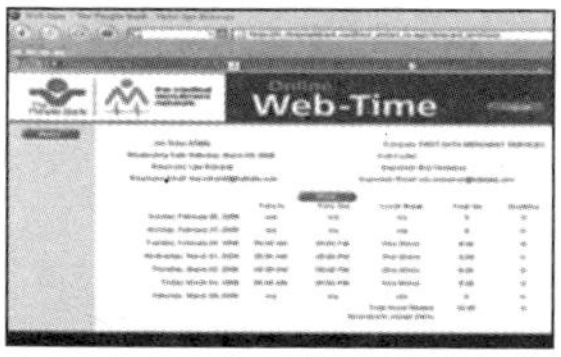

FIGURE 7.6
An excerpt from the solution section of Lisa Richards's white paper on "Web-Time."

USEFUL STRATEGIES TO INCREASE THE EFFECTIVENESS OF YOUR WHITE PAPER

Stand Back from Your Subject Matter and Summarize the Key Points That Newcomers Need to Know to Appreciate the Issue, Product, or Service

Sometimes when we are too familiar with a topic, we assume that everyone else is equally knowledgeable, so we start the discussion at too high a level. To ensure that you include contextual and background information, outline the basic problem or requirements. For example, for a computer-based product, list the following basics:

- Is it a hardware, software, or a web-based solution?
- What support equipment or conditions are necessary?
- What platform is it designed for?
- What language is it written in or does it assume some knowledge of?
- Who will find this product useful?

If you address these kinds of issues clearly in the white paper, readers can quickly and easily assess whether to keep reading: if the product is compatible with their current system, they will be interested in your argument; if not, they will move on.

Assume Your Reader Is a Newcomer to the Subject

If you are addressing newcomers, you assume that they are not aware of the significant issues associated with this topic: your discussion should fill them in on the key points they should know. Once they are familiar with the basic issues, they will be equipped to follow and appreciate the argument that you build to support your solution.

Describe the Problem in Specific and Personalized Terms

One expert recommends using a case study or narrative as an interesting and attention-grabbing way to set up the problem that you raise or that your product or service solves. Case studies employ characters and situations that make the problem come to life: a narrative approach is more likely to draw in readers, who will want to keep reading to find out how the problem is resolved. This approach also allows you to present a fully developed example of how to solve the problem set up in the case.

---

1. Potential Risks of AR/XR Technology:

AR apps gather extensive intimate personal data, e.g., biometric data (facial expressions, retina patterns), personal behavior (walking gait, arm movements, speech patterns), individual's movements (daily activities, schedules, favored routes).

Huge amounts of data are gathered and stored: Who can access this data? How are they using it?

How secure is this personal and private data?

How does frequent and lengthy use of AR/XR affect users' mental health?

When AR/XR can be used to create and record events that never happened, how does the viewer know whether this record is "real" or fabricated?

What are the physical risks associated with using AR/XR?

Does it violate individual employees' privacy rights that industry is already using XR to monitor and record employees' work performance?

2. Reader Motivations:

To keep themselves informed about potential benefits and risks to children's well-being.

To raise/educate children who are healthy in mind and body.

To raise/educate children whose persons, as well as personal data, are kept safe from misuse or abuse.

Keep users of these apps safe in the short and long term.

Make decisions in the users' best interests.

Support and influence national policy to regulate data collection associated with XR apps.

FIGURE 7.7

Blackwell's analysis of potential risks of AR/XR technology and target readers' motivations.

1. Risk: Company's Use of and Access to Users' Biometric Data. If AR/XR gaming apps collect users' biometric data, who has access to it, and what does the company do with it beyond that one-time use? Parents and educators must learn what happens to the data generated by a specific app, so they can make an informed decision about whether their children can safely use it (reader benefit). (Reader Motivation: Stay informed and make good decisions to protect children.)

2. Risk: Data Breaches Are Unavoidable. Users' data, even when securely maintained, may be compromised, risking users' long-term privacy/safety. Parents and educators should develop protocols for making decisions about whether children can safely use a particular AR/XR app (reader benefit). (Reader Motivation: Keep app users safe in the short and long term.)

3. Risk: AR/XR Apps Allow Users to Create and Record Events that Never Happened. These events appear "real" but are not. Parents and educators need to ensure children develop strategies to evaluate the accuracy and truthfulness of the records they encounter online (reader benefit). (Reader Motivation: Children are healthy in mind and body.)

FIGURE 7.8
Blackwell generates a series of reader benefits by connecting the list of risks she decides are most important with her anticipated reader motivations.

If You Are Describing a Product or Service, Explain How It Works and How Its Features Benefit the Reader

When you describe how the product or service works, detail clearly and accurately the special features that make it useful and desirable. Once you have described the special features, *then* show readers how those features provide specific benefits. Describing reader benefits helps readers to imagine the ways in which the product or service might be useful to them. If you are discussing an issue, explain how the key elements of your critique are relevant to the needs or concerns of readers and elaborate the implications.

In Your Argument, Link Reader Motivations with Risks

To create a persuasive argument—that is, an argument that moves readers to act—Blackwell then has to develop points that clearly link the risks she has identified with AR/XR applications and those values or needs that motivate her target readers. In Figure 7.8, Blackwell creates three brief arguments that explicitly link the risks with her readers' needs and suggests how readers can achieve their goals and mitigate the identified risk. These suggestions are READER BENEFITS— they show readers how they will benefit by taking the suggested action. When readers understand how the suggested action will help them achieve their goals, they are likely to do what is suggested.

Align Product Features with Reader Motivations to Create Reader Benefits

In her white paper (refer back to Figures 7.5 and 7.6), Lisa Richards likewise includes several well-developed reader benefits as she explains the "Solution" section of her paper. (See Figure 7.9.) She notes that the Web-Time program provides these benefits:

1. Security for workers
2. Reduced interruptions for supervisors
3. Increased efficiency in the workplace
4. Cost savings for both the temp agency and the client company

---

In addition to all of the practical features that Web-Time boasts, this system provides security for workers, who can rest assured that they will be paid consistently on a weekly basis (depending on the pay period specified by the temp agency) and that their pay will be an accurate reflection of the hours that they have submitted. Supervisors also benefit from Web-Time by being able to complete their tasks with less interruption, freeing office equipment (i.e., fax machines) to be used for other business purposes and minimizing the risk of potential problems such as their employees not being paid as a result of timesheets getting lost among other faxes.

Since implementing Web-Time, the supervisors have been able to schedule their noon hour on Mondays to scroll through all of the timesheets of their employees and verify hours. They no longer have to be interrupted for signatures when they may have been focusing on another task at the time.

Web-Time is superior to other forms of hour tracking as it is efficient, allows the company to maintain solid productivity without interruption, and is financially sound for businesses. This saves the temp agency money by reducing its costs since the agency does not have to print sufficient timesheets for employees, distribute them (normally by mail, which then adds the cost of a stamp), and then print one faxed timesheet per employee. The reduction in paper waste is also environmentally friendly.

FIGURE 7.9
The reader benefits that Lisa Richards describes in explaining her solution to the problem.

IN-CLASS EXERCISE 7.1

Converting Product Features to Reader Benefits

Select a product or device that you know well and like well enough that you could sell its merits to someone else.

1. Generate a list of at least 10 features that the product has that make it useful and desirable.
2. Brainstorm a list of potential motivations.
3. Create a third list of the features (listed in #1) that can meet some of the motivations (listed in #2).
4. Finally, develop as many reader benefits as you can from your analysis.

Write two paragraphs, one that describes three or four of the most important features of the device and one that elaborates some of the reader benefits of owning it.

One Expert's Helpful Hint

Here is one pointer that expert writers of white papers recommend to increase your chances of success. Wade Nelson recommends that you mention one or two limitations in your product description so that you present a balanced view. He notes that, by acknowledging some limitations, you also add more persuasive weight to your claims for the product's advantages.

Following this advice, Lisa also includes the following limitations at the end of her discussion of the solution to show her balanced view of the situation she describes: "A limitation that Web-Time could potentially face is servers becoming overloaded when multiple employees try to log into the service simultaneously. Also, should the website be down for whatever reason, they will not be able to submit their hours online. These limitations have not occurred yet, but, in a worst-case scenario, the paper timesheet is a fallback option." These points help to strengthen her persuasive case.

MAJOR PROJECT 7.2

WRITE A WHITE PAPER

Select a new product or device that you know something about, and write a white paper introducing it to readers who will find this innovation helpful. Potential topics could include educational technologies to encourage online discussion during class lectures, apps for helping students with their writing, and online meeting software.

LAB ASSIGNMENT 7.2

USER TEST YOUR WHITE PAPER DRAFT

Bring three or four copies of your draft white paper to class with you. In groups of three people, user test your drafts, one draft at a time. Distribute a copy of your draft to the members of your group and have each person read it aloud, one at a time. Take notes, as first one reads the paper and then the other, to record places where readers pause or stumble over the wording. Use the discussion above to help you plan and execute your usability test.

RECOMMENDATION REPORTS

The recommendation report is the written outcome that often follows a study or research into a particular problem. In a recommendation report, the technical communicator (or engineer) describes the problem and then presents several possible solutions that he or she has devised based on extensive research. If the writer has been asked only to recommend several solutions, the report ends with a neutral description of the possibilities. If the writer has been asked to solve the problem, then he or she will generally end by recommending one solution over the others, explaining what makes it superior. A variation on the recommendation report is the feasibility report, which discusses the viability of applying one recommended solution to a problem.

REPORT STRUCTURE

- Memo or letter of transmittal
- Title page
- Executive summary or abstract
- Recommendations
- Report body
- Conclusions
- Notes, references, appendices

Memo or Letter of Transmittal

Usually, the memo or letter of transmittal is separate from the report, but it accompanies the report to provide a context for the reader, especially the reader who requested the report. It is usually directed toward your boss or the individual who requested the research.

Use general conventions when deciding whether you should use a memo or a letter: for an internal report going to your supervisor, use a memo; for an external report, submitted to an organization from your consulting firm, use a letter. See Figure 7.10 for a sample letter of transmittal, written by Michael Trottier, after a work term as a building inspector for an engineering company. The report from which this letter is taken was prepared for a writing class that was part of his degree program; the actual report submitted to the clients would be longer and more detailed than the version prepared for the class. The letter or memo of transmittal should communicate the following information:

- Transmit the report—that is, formally release or publish this document.
- Summarize the conclusions and recommendations from the report. Usually the conclusions and recommendations are stated in one-sentence summaries that signal the direction of the report but don't provide any details to explain.
- Explain any problems you encountered and how you solved them. If you ran into any minor problems while you were researching and writing the report, describe those in the letter or memo of transmittal and explain how you solved them.
- Thank those who helped you with the report. In a sentence or two, acknowledge the help of any co-workers or individuals whose efforts made your work on the report easier or better.
- Point out any additional research, if it is needed. If you found over the course of the project that additional research should be done but was outside the scope of the project, also include this advice in the letter or memo of transmittal.
- Thank the reader for the chance to do this work. Note the ways in which you found the work of benefit. This kind of closing establishes a positive conclusion for the letter and helps the reader to anticipate the rest of the report.
- Offer to answer questions. The final point in the letter or memo of transmittal should be an offer to answer any questions. Include your contact information, so the reader can easily reach you should he or she have questions.

Title Page

The title page should be the first bound page in the report, and it should present this information:

- The full title of the report
- The names of the individuals who prepared the report
- For whom it was prepared .
- The release date of the report

July 5, 20xx

Dear Client:

Re. Home Inspection
947 Woodbury Dr., Springfield

ValuSpec Home Inspection Service has completed a visual inspection of the property and building at the address above. Thank you for choosing ValuSpec, and we appreciate the chance to work with you at this time. The enclosed report provides you with extensive information about the general condition of this property after a visual examination of the accessible areas of the house, based on the enclosed Inspection Agreement. Please note that no aspect of the home was dismantled, so the inspection judgments are based only on the evidence visible without further probing.

We found three major areas of the home and property that you would want to address within a year or two of purchasing this property. There are a number of minor issues, and they are detailed in the report. We recommend that you complete the following at your earliest convenience:

1. Replace the roof.
2. Improve ventilation in interior to reduce overall humidity levels.
3. Improve drainage around base of foundation at southeast and northeast corners of the house.

The inspection began at 9 a.m. and concluded at 11:30 a.m. on June 27, 20xx. The current owners of the property were in residence at the time, so our inspection was limited to a visual examination with little moving of personal effects.

I would like to thank Robert Stafford, P. Eng., who allowed me to accompany him during the inspection as part of my responsibilities as a student worker at ValuSpec. He also reviewed a draft of this report, and his comments were helpful in sharpening my analysis and clarifying my explanations, especially of obvious humidity problems on the premises.

Again, thank you for the opportunity to undertake this inspection. It has made a valuable contribution to my education as a civil engineer.

If you have questions or concerns after reading this report, please contact me at mtrottie@gmail.com or telephone me at 123-456-7890.

Sincerely,

Michael Trottier

Michael Trottier

FIGURE 7.10
The letter of transmittal for a home inspection report written by Michael Trottier during a work term at ValuSpec Home Inspections. This report was written as an assignment for a writing class as part of Trottier's degree. Please note that the actual report submitted to the homeowners was significantly longer and more detailed.

Executive Summary or Abstract

Executive summaries or abstracts are generally two or three pages. They provide a brief but clear overview of the report. Busy executives should be able to read the executive summary or abstract and know what the report is about. Abstracts should summarize the report recommendations and explain why these recommendations are made. They outline the topics discussed and the depth of each discussion. They are organized to inform readers about what they need to know; they should not repeat the organization of ideas in the report itself. Figure 7.11 reproduces part of an executive summary.

EXECUTIVE SUMMARY

Conclusions

Overall the dwelling and yard are in fair condition. There appear to be no major structural problems that would affect a potential purchaser's decision to buy this property. That said, the house is 18 years old, and some of its systems do show wear and tear equal to a residential property of this age.

Recommendations

We recommend that the client consider the following maintenance projects within the next two years:

1. **Replace the roof.** Currently, the roof consists of one layer of asphalt composite shingles. Noted were worn, curling shingles; loose or missing gravel; and evidence of patching. We were unable to determine whether these repairs were effective. Based on these observations and information obtained from the current owner, the shingles are nearly 18 years old. The shingles currently in place average 15–20 years, and they show normal wear and tear for their age. The age of the roofing membrane appears to be reaching its useful life, so we recommend that the client plan to replace it in the near future.

2. **Improve interior ventilation to reduce overall humidity levels**. We noted a potential environmental issue with the presence of mold on interior portions of several windows in the home and basement. A more intrusive examination would be needed to determine the scope and nature of the mold growth. We recommend removing all sources of moisture: install or repair kitchen and bathroom exhaust fans; disconnect furnace humidifier, and use dehumidifier to remove excess moisture; seal the building envelope to prevent water entering from the outside. If mold persists after completing these actions, consult a qualified mold abatement contractor for additional evaluation and treatment options to ensure safe air quality indoors.

3. **Improve grading around building foundation**. We saw evidence of some leakage around the windows in the basement. Ground levels around the foundation also show some compression against the concrete where rainwater and other moisture could pool, presenting a potential leakage problem. We recommend redoing the grading by building up earth in compression areas. The earth against the house should slope away so that water will run away rather than pool around the foundation.

The report provides a detailed discussion of all of the major systems in the house and evaluates their condition, making suggestions where appropriate about solutions that the client should undertake to improve conditions. Minor problems to be aware of include several inoperable systems: electrostatic air cleaner on the furnace, garage door opener....

FIGURE 7.11
Part of the executive summary that Trottier prepared for his report.

Recommendations

The next section of the report (usually on a separate page from what has gone before) presents the recommendations. In this section, you list the action items that you recommend to solve the problem or problems identified in the report. After each recommendation, describe your rationale for making this suggestion. This is the only place where your recommendations are discussed fully, so include everything readers will need to know to understand and make decisions about your recommendations.

Note: It is crucial that you connect your recommendations directly to the results and discussion that you present in the report. Refer to the results and discussion section when you make a recommendation so that the reader can see why you made that recommendation.

Main Part of the Report (Note: Do Not Use "Body" as a Report Heading)

The sections discussed previously are all preliminary to the actual report. Your goal in the report is to assemble all of the research that you did to explain what you see as the most viable solutions to the problem that prompted this project in the first place. So the report should address the following general topics:

- An outline and overview of the problem
- Your purpose in undertaking the report
- How you collected the information that forms the basis of this report
- The results and analysis of your research
- A discussion of what you see as the findings of your research

Although the content of every report will be different, there are a number of rhetorical moves that you want to make in each part of the body of your report, whatever its topic.

INTRODUCTION

In the introduction, provide a brief overview of the problem that initiated the report. Explain any background information that readers need to understand the topic. If there are technical terms that are unavoidable, define these terms clearly and concisely. If there are several specialized terms or concepts that readers need defined, consider including a glossary or list of terms at the back of the report, and direct readers to it in the introduction.

Explain the significance of the problem, its cost in terms of money or time, and the importance of finding an appropriate solution. Even if your main reader (your supervisor) already understands the problem and agrees that it exists, you should still provide a coherent account of the problem because most reports have a much wider circulation than the original individual who requested them. For this reason, you should include in the introduction any information that will educate readers who have little knowledge about the immediate problem, so they can understand and evaluate your assessment in the rest of the report.

Depending upon the seriousness of the problem and the complexity of the background, your introduction can be anywhere from two or three paragraphs to several pages. Your goal is to provide all the information readers need clearly and concisely.

Figure 7.12 presents the introduction of Trottier's home inspection report where he summarizes the reason for writing the report as well as its limitations and goals. The introduction is brief because a home inspection report generally deals with a well-recognized problem. The home inspection and the report that follow generally arise from a real estate transaction; a potential buyer wants to uncover any costly structural or system-related problems that the seller has not disclosed but that the buyer will have to repair or replace upon purchasing the property. By identifying the report as a home inspection report, the writer communicates the context for the report and for anticipating the types of problems that it solves. For this reason, Trottier doesn't need to explain further after he identifies the location of the property, names the individual who commissioned the inspection, and defines any specialized terms.

Assess the amount of detail that your report will require. You may need to provide several pages of details to explain the nature of the problem if you are writing a different kind of recommendation report than the home inspection report. Given the broad nature of the potential situations that your recommendation report may address, you need to analyze your subject matter, your readers, and your situation to determine how much introduction your readers will need to understand your topic. These guidelines and strategies are general, and we intend that you adapt the relevant ones to your particular project and omit the ones that seem redundant or ill-fitting.

LITERATURE REVIEW

In academic or research reports, you may decide or be required to include a section called a literature review. This is essentially a specialized form of the background section. In it you report on your reading of what has been written on the topic or subject of your report. The key skills here are your ability to identify trends in the research and then produce a summary of these main trends or lines of thought about the topic. In the case of the home report, Trottier could have produced a section that outlined the main challenges faced by homeowners in Winnipeg. For example, flooding has been a problem historically. Trottier could have written an overview of articles and reports drawn from realtor websites, newspapers, the city's website, and other sources. In the case of an academic topic, literature reviews identify major trends in the research on a topic and then place the report topic within the context of these trends.

PURPOSE

Under the heading of purpose, you outline briefly why the report was undertaken and state its goal.

INTRODUCTION

This report provides information about the condition of the home and property at 947 Woodbury Dr. It was written in response to a request by Charles Fields for an inspection of the home in connection with the possible purchase of the property. He requested that we examine the systems within the house with the goal of identifying any that needed repair or replacement, with an emphasis on evaluating the potential seriousness and costliness of addressing any structural or system-related problems that were noted.

This report details the condition of the home as it was observed during the inspection on June 27, 20xx. As is routine in reports of this nature, we have summarized the overall condition of the house before detailing the specific condition of the various systems of the house. The discussion moves from the exterior of the building to the lower level and then to the main level. The major systems demanding immediate attention are summarized in the Recommendations section of the report. More minor problems are noted during the general description of the survey results.

Please note that the following terms are used in the report:

S = serviceable, meaning the materials and workmanship associated with the part being inspected are acceptable, and it is in generally satisfactory condition.
N = not applicable, meaning the part does not exist or apply to the property.

Also note that the point of reference given to locate a particular component is the front exterior of the building, facing the main entrance (e.g., the sump pump is located in the lower level at the rear right side).

Limitations

Please remember that the personal effects of the current owner occasionally limited the scope of the inspection because the inspection team was unable to undertake extensive moving of these effects. However, we have noted in the report those instances when the belongings limited the examination.

Purpose

The purpose of this report is to evaluate the overall condition of the building and property at 947 Woodbury Dr. in Springfield, and to assess the extent of any structural or system-related problems that will require repair or replacement.

FIGURE 7.12
The opening of the body of the inspection report by Trottier. Note that he has added the section "Limitations" to draw his readers' attention to one of the limitations of the inspection—the presence of the current owner's belongings, which occasionally prevented thorough inspection of a room or closet. He added this heading because he was concerned that embedding this point inside the introduction might make it easy to miss.

METHODS

In the third section, the method, describe how you collected the information presented in the report. If you interviewed individuals, surveyed large groups, read published studies and books on the subject matter, and so on, include these details. Your aim is to show that you did a competent, thorough job of studying the problem and looking for a range of viable solutions. If you conducted survey research on which to base your results, describe briefly how you selected the sample population and developed the questions that you used. Include a copy of the survey in the report appendix, and refer your readers to it for additional information. If your results are based on statistical analysis, explain how you calculated your results. The goal here is to provide readers with information about how the study was conducted, so they can judge your work's thoroughness and quality.

RESULTS

This section summarizes the data and results that your methods produced. Include tables, graphs, charts, and figures to present and emphasize statistical or numerical information. Visualizations allow you to present processed rather than raw data, but include raw numbers, as appropriate, in the appendix. Present and highlight the data that support your argument in the report. Presumably, your solutions are based on the results of your research, so present results to lay a foundation for your explanation of your decisions (which will be discussed in detail in the section that follows).

This section presents your results but *not* your interpretation of the results. Discuss the meaning of the results at length in the next section, the "Discussion." The results and interpretation are discussed separately, so readers can focus on the nature and quality of your research data before they must digest what these data mean. In some ways, you can use the results section to anticipate and begin to support your discussion by laying out and emphasizing those results that are most relevant to the solutions that you intend to propose.

DISCUSSION

As noted previously, this section is the opportunity to discuss your results thoroughly and to explain the thinking that led to you choosing your recommended solution. Highlight what you see as the most important findings and show why they are the most important. Then discuss the implications of these findings— that is, the ways in which they lead inevitably to the solution proposed in the recommendations.

CONCLUSIONS

The final section of the body of the report presents your conclusions. In this part, you summarize the main points that you want readers to take away from the report. Never introduce new topics or information in the conclusion. The ideas that you express here should all be drawn from what you have said elsewhere in the report. To emphasize your conclusions, present them in a bulleted or numbered list.

Notes, References, Appendices

The final sections of the report are comprised of any notes, the references, and any appendices. If you used published sources, such as articles, books, data sets, or websites, include these in your "References" section after notes but before appendices. If you have data, or questionnaires, or computer printouts of statistical analyses, then include these in an "Appendix" or an "Appendices" section as the final part of the report. Consider how numerous the appended information is when deciding how to arrange it. If this information is fairly limited, think about gathering it together in one appendix. If you have many pages and various types of data, consider putting each grouping in its own appendix. At the relevant point in the body of the report, refer readers to this appended material, indicating which appendix contains which type of information.

WRITING A RECOMMENDATION REPORT

Write a recommendation report based on a topic of your choice. First, identify a problem that someone you know (or work with) has that can be solved by a technological solution. Conduct the necessary research to figure out which technological solution is the best one. Based on your research, write a recommendation report for your reader that describes the problem and recommends the solution that you believe is the best one.

Many of the topics that are covered in this book will be important to consider as you write your report, including document design, adding visuals where appropriate to present statistical or technical data, organizing information, and making your writing clear for specific audiences. Follow the format outlined in this chapter on how to structure a recommendation report.

Purpose and Audience

Before you begin, you should have a clear sense of who your primary and secondary readers are for the report. Include the background information that they will need to understand your discussion, and tailor your arguments to match those that your readers will find convincing and compelling. Also make sure that you understand why you are writing this report and what main points you want to convey to your readers.

Use the outline below to structure your report, and draw on the rhetorical appeals discussed in Chapter 4, "Writing Technical Prose," to develop and explain the solutions that you found for the problem that you identified and analyzed:

- Letter or memo of transmittal
- Title page
- Executive summary or abstract
- Recommendations
- Body of report (introduction, scope, methods, results, discussion)
- Conclusions
- Works cited or references
- Appendices

CHAPTER EIGHT

Reporting Technical Information

THE LABORATORY REPORT

Each field that uses the laboratory report has its own specific requirements about how to write one well. This section will *not* detail the specifics of biology, chemistry, physics, or engineering lab reports because doing so is beyond the scope of this book. However, this section *will* introduce you, generally, to the rhetorical strategies and genre requirements that make a good lab report. Your instructors in the specific fields will provide you with details about their specialties' preferences, which you can then use in adapting the more general information here.

There are two parts to writing a good laboratory report. One is the report itself, but the initial step that directly affects your report quality is how well you record your experiment in the laboratory notebook while doing the experiment. For this reason, this section reviews the basics of keeping a good laboratory notebook and then describes how to transform the notes into a laboratory report. Generally, the laboratory report is an academic exercise in which students gain experience replicating common experiments while they learn how to use equipment, perform common laboratory-based activities, and report their results in written form. The lab report points students toward understanding the genre of the experimental report and the fundamental ways in which it is different from something like an essay or a recommendation report.

THE LABORATORY NOTEBOOK

Experimental descriptions originate in the laboratory notebook. Laboratory reports rest on a foundation of experimental evidence, first recorded in the notebook, so they are only as good as the records made during the experiment. While you are conducting the experiment, you should be recording clear and detailed notes about the following:

- Your actions
- Your observations
- Your thoughts

If you make detailed notes, the laboratory report will be much easier to write later because it won't depend on your short-term memory. The key elements here are that you record this information as it takes place, in a systematic fashion and in a permanent place—the laboratory notebook.

Your Lab Notebook and Scientific Integrity

Your laboratory notebook should have the following qualities:

- It should be a bound volume. Experts recommend that you use a bound notebook. Don't use a loose-leaf binder for your notebook because the pages can fall out easily or be moved out of sequence. Don't use a spiral notebook because pages can be removed without it being noticeable.
- All of the pages should be numbered and dated in sequence.
- All entries should be in waterproof, non-erasable ink.
- Don't leave blank pages.

These qualities all have to do with scientific integrity. It is critical that the notes you take during an experiment are as accurate and clear as you can make them. You can change your notes during the experiment as long as you record what you changed and why, but they should not be altered later or even crossed out beyond a single line drawn through the entry so that it remains legible. While this degree of care and accuracy may seem excessive at your level of study, remember that these activities are establishing good habits. If you get used to keeping an accurate and careful record of your actions during an experiment, you will not have to unlearn bad habits later, when the stakes of having inaccurate observations and fudged data might be much higher and more serious. For example, in an industrial lab, the notebook is a legal record of discovery. If the researchers maintain a high level of detail and accuracy in the notebook, it can stand up in a court of law to prove what was done and when it was done. In disputes over who was the first to discover a new idea or who is entitled to the patent on it, the notebook is central to the discussion of the legal issues.

In higher education settings, instructors often prescribe how to write laboratory entries as part of the course lab manual, sometimes setting out strict penalties for not following the requirements. They specify how they want data kept in a notebook, and their requirements usually include rules about content, structure, level of detail, and quality of the descriptions and written text. For example, one chemistry instructor informs students of these rules:

1. Buy the required laboratory notebook at the bookstore. It must be formatted for duplicate pages and recording page numbers. [Duplicate pages are used in pharmaceutical research.] Do not tear out any pages—not a single one. [These points are relevant to training students to work in a patent or research lab.]
2. The lab notebook must have a table of contents. Leave the first *two full pages* blank so that you can fill in the name and page numbers of each experiment as you enter it into the book.

3. Keep your lab notebook up to date. Add to the table of contents with each new experiment. Your TA [teaching assistant] or instructor will check your lab book after every second or third experiment.

4. When you are in the laboratory, write only in this notebook. Do not jot down ideas on scrap paper.

5. Write all relevant information related to the experiments on the right page of the notebook. Record in your notebook all data and other information needed to complete the lab assignment.

6. Write all entries in blue or black *ink*. Do not record entries first in pencil and then trace over them later in pen. Do not erase any entries. Marks will be deducted for pencil, overwritten, or erased entries.

7. Use correct units for all data. Clearly label all of your data, and tabulate them so that readers reviewing your notebook can easily understand these data.

Note that these rules all have to do with maintaining the integrity of the information in the notebook. They also try to ensure that students conduct the experiment as intended rather than trying to "back engineer" the data to get the expected results. Although these rules may seem prescriptive, they reflect procedures followed in industry to maintain the integrity of data developed there. Industrial laboratories often have rules that notebook pages must be signed and researchers must have important results and data witnessed to verify accuracy and reliability. Why all this concern about the veracity of scientific or experimental data? All records must be accurate and truthful in case they become evidence in legal disputes. For example, in lawsuits over intellectual property and patent issues, the dates, details, and raw data from research become crucial evidence to support claims in law courts.

How Should You Organize the Information in Your Notebook?

Some instructors will direct you to leave the first two or three pages of the notebook blank, so that later, when you have filled the rest of the pages, you can come back and add a table of contents to help you (and others) locate the data for specific experiments.

Usually, experiment notes are divided into two parts: the introduction (or pre-lab portion) and the narrative (or the in-lab section). To reduce the amount of work that you need to complete during the lab itself, you can prepare the pre-lab in advance of actually conducting the experiment. See Figure 8.1 for an example from Aaron Goldberg's lab notebook prepared for a second-year chemistry experiment, "Gravimetric Determination of Calcium as $CaC_2O_4 \cdot H_2O$." Note that the left page contains the pre-lab information, while the right page displays the narrative—the observations and measurements made during the experiment in the lab.

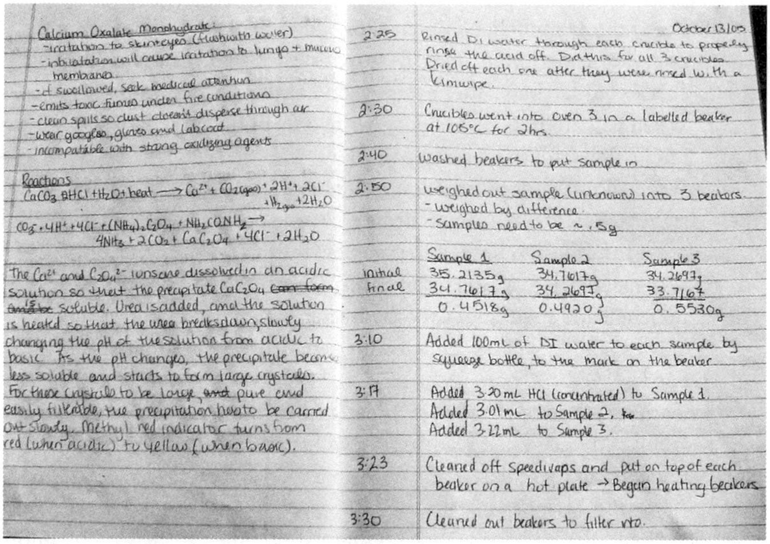

FIGURE 8.1

Goldberg's lab notebook from the chemistry experiment, "Gravimetric Determination of Calcium as $CaC_2O_4 \cdot H_2O$." The left page presents the pre-lab or introduction while the right page presents the narrative—the observations and measurements made during the experiment in the lab.

INTRODUCTION (PRE-LAB CONTEXT)

In the introduction, include the kinds of details that establish a context for the experiment:

- Title
- Location and date
- Goal of the experiment
- Citations of relevant background literature
- Description of materials used and information about safety data
- Account of experimental conditions and reactions
- Description of experimental procedure you plan to follow (not to be confused with a description of the procedure that you actually followed, which appears in the narrative section)

NARRATIVE (IN LAB)

Write a Detailed Account

The narrative section provides a detailed account of the experiment—the way that you actually conducted it. This means that you should pause every few minutes throughout the experiment to record clearly and accurately what you have just finished doing. Describe your actions and your observations. This level of detail helps you reconstruct the activity when you write the laboratory report later. The goal is to have more information in your notebook account of the experiment than you will need when you actually write the report.

Separate Speculation from Reality

If you have ideas about how to explain what is happening, make sure that you distinguish the way you record them from your method of recording the actual happenings, so you separate the real from the speculative. When you write the report later, you want to avoid confusing what actually happened with what you thought you were seeing at the time or what you hoped might be happening.

Record Every Measurement

The notebook is the appropriate place to record all of your raw data. Even though you will find some of your measurements irrelevant to the experiment when you later interpret the data, you still want to have a permanent record of everything associated with the experiment. You should also include any sources of error that may have affected your results and made them different from what you expected. Preserve all measurements in your notebook so that, at a later date, if you need to correct a calculation or check some aspect of your results, they are available. You may find that these apparently irrelevant data are what you should have used earlier, and if you had discarded them, the experiment would be worthless.

WRITING THE LABORATORY REPORT

Writing the laboratory report is the final stage in the process of research, the stage at which you interpret and communicate the results of your study. The report provides an account of the experiment or experiments that you conducted in the lab, and it is a permanent record of your activities and observations. Other individuals should be able to repeat your activities as described in the report and arrive at similar results and observations (that is, your results should be replicable or repeatable).

The laboratory report is used in higher education to assess and evaluate your performance in the lab. It is also an exercise that helps you to learn how to process the raw data that you collect, analyze data into an interpretation, and then present that interpretation in the report as an argument supported with data. It also provides a chance for you to evaluate your knowledge of the topic and argue the significance of your work.

Before you can begin writing the report, you must decide what information and data you should include. Spend some time analyzing your data by applying the theories and principles that drove the research to the data and observations that you collected. This will help you make sense of your findings. After the experiment is complete, you should have more insight into the events of the experiment than you did while you were in the middle of it. Use this insight to help you distinguish the useful data from the erroneous or irrelevant. You may also need to decide whether or not you should include any of the erroneous or irrelevant data to help clarify the meaningful results.

Do not be tempted to adjust any of your data at this point to improve your results. Tampering with your data is a grievous sin in scientific research at any level. A lab report is assumed to be based on truthful data, and your findings are taken as facts based on truth. Making adjustments to the data undermines the integrity of the knowledge you present in your report and, through it, of the whole scientific enterprise. Even findings that seem impossible should be acknowledged, never altered or discarded.

To begin writing you need to have the following:

- Data (drawn from the narrative in your lab notebook)
- Results calculated from the raw data of the notebook
- Knowledge of the theories or principles underlying the experiment
- References or sources for the theories or principles

Format of the Lab Report

The laboratory report has an established format. All of the information presented in it should appear in one of the headings listed:

- Title (and author[s])
- Introduction
- Procedure and materials
- Results
- Discussion
- References

TITLE (AND AUTHOR[S])

Choose a short but informative title for your report. It should reflect the content of the paper and catch the reader's interest. List the keywords from the subject matter of the experiment and include them in your title.

Don't forget to also include such information as your name (and the names of collaborators, if applicable), the course and section number, the day and time of the lab, and the date that you conducted the experiment. Your instructor may also request additional information on the title page of your report: be sure to include it too.

INTRODUCTION

The introduction of the report should accomplish several goals. It should explain the purpose of the experiment and include enough background information on the subject matter to establish the context for the experiment. That is, readers should gain a general but clear sense of what you did, why you did it, and why it matters. The introduction should be as brief as possible while still including all relevant information:

- Clearly state the purpose of the experiment.
- Describe the nature and scope of the problem being investigated.
- Review relevant literature to give readers a context for your experiment.
- Limit the background to what readers need to know.
- Identify clearly how your data refer to what is known and not known about the topic.
- Include any definitions or principles that readers need to understand the experiment.

- State methods of the experiment only if they are part of the purpose (e.g., evaluating two techniques).
- Briefly summarize the principal results of the experiment.

Figure 8.2 is a sample introduction taken from Kavita Patel's microbiology lab report. Given space limitations in this volume, only part (three-quarters) of the introduction is reproduced here.

THE EFFECTS OF TEMPERATURE AND PH ON ENCOURAGING AND DETERRING THE GROWTH OF BACTERIA VS. FUNGUS

Introduction

This experiment was done to determine the optimal temperature and pH conditions for different micro-organisms. These two environmental factors have the greatest impact on the growth of a micro-organism, which makes them both important and straightforward to study. It is important to know the optimal temperature and pH for the growth of different bacteria and fungi because they both affect our food and our health. In this experiment, the amount of growth of micro-organisms was determined using a spectrophotometer as well as visually. Using both methods also highlights the strengths and weaknesses of both techniques.

For the determination of optimum temperature, four bacteria and two fungi were used, and for the determination of optimum pH, three bacteria and one fungus were used. The bacteria used grow at different optimal temperatures, but were all capable of growing well on the same nutrient agar plates or nutrient broth solutions. Similarly, the fungi used in the temperature determination were both grown on Sabouraud's agar. Every micro-organism that was used for this experiment can be found in some type of food, either as an aid to processing it or as spoilage.

Temperature is the most influential environmental condition that affects cell growth and survival (Madigan *et al.*, 2003). At the optimum temperature for a specific micro-organism, its biochemical reactions run quickly, allowing the cell to grow at its maximum rate. This is the optimal growth range for temperature for a specific organism. If the temperature is increased too far past this point, the maximum temperature of the organism is reached. This is the temperature at which the micro-organism's enzymes begin to be denatured by the heat, prohibiting the growth of the cell. The minimum temperature is the lowest temperature at which the organism can grow. Below this temperature, the reactions within the cell occur too slowly, and the cell membrane begins to gel, prohibiting growth (Madigan *et al.*, 2003). The optimal growth range of temperatures that micro-organisms grow best at can be anywhere from below 0°C to above 100°C (Madigan *et al.*, 2003). Increasing or decreasing the temperature of an organism's environment to within the micro-organism's optimal temperature range encourages growth. Conversely, if the environmental temperature is moved not only out of the optimal range for the organism but also past the maximum or minimum temperature, the micro-organism can no longer survive. The closer that the environmental temperature gets to the maximum or minimum for a specific organism, the more growth is deterred.

FIGURE 8.2

The introduction section of a microbiology lab report. Only three-quarters of the section is reproduced here because of space limitations.

METHODS AND MATERIALS

This experiment was performed as outlined in the *Biology 140L Fundamentals of Microbiology Lab Manual Fall Term* 2020, experiments 20 and 21, from pages 77–81.

No changes were made to this procedure.

FIGURE 8.3
The procedures and materials section of Patel's microbiology lab.

In the introduction, Patel has briefly identified the purpose of the experiment (to determine the optimal environment for growing micro-organisms) and the reason this knowledge is important (micro-organism growth affects human health and food safety). She then lists the micro-organisms that were studied and some background or theory about the experiment (temperature is the most important factor in promoting or preventing micro-organism growth).

PROCEDURES AND MATERIALS

In this section, describe the procedure you followed to obtain the results that you present. This description should contain enough information to enable someone else to perform the same experiment successfully but still be clear and concise.

Some science courses will provide you with a manual that details the procedure you should follow for some of the experiments. If this is the case, then often you won't need to detail your procedures in the lab report. Instead, you can just refer the reader to the procedures outlined in the manual, as Patel has done in Figure 8.3. Cite fully the procedure that you reference (i.e., title, course number, author, year of publication of manual, and page numbers of the lab you are referring to). However, if you deviated from any part of the manual's description, you should note and describe in this section the changes that you made during the experiment.

As with the introduction, aim for clear and concise prose in this section of the report.

RESULTS

The results section presents your findings. First, describe how you got your results, and, second, explain the results' significance (i.e., what they mean).

This organizational structure means that the first half of this section presents comprehensible processed data. So organize the information, perhaps by placing it in tables or by laying out the critical calculations upon which your interpretation is based. The finished results (as you present them in this section) should support the interpretation that you have decided to present for your data.

The laboratory report should include all of the data that you collected from the experiment. However, the raw data should be assembled in an "Appendix" at the end. Also include in the appendix any computer printouts or instrument tracings that you used to derive data for the experiment.

Occasionally, you may have to use in your report data collected by someone else. If this is the case, you *must* state the sources of your data, giving credit to the collector. Passing off someone else's raw data as your own is fraudulent and an academic offence.

Organize and Present Your Data

There are three ways to present data so they are easily understood and processed by readers. Select the method that best presents the point about your data that you want to make. Compare some of your data to other data you collected; if appropriate, compare your data to that gathered by others in your class.

RESULTS

Table 1. Growth of Micro-organisms under Different Temperature Conditions

Organism	4–6°C	20–25°C	37°C	55°C	Optimal (°C)
Staphylococcus aureus	–	++ yellow	+++	–	37
Serratia marcescens	+	+++ red	+++	–	20–25
Pseudomonas fluorescens	++	+++	–	–	20–25
Bacillus stearothermophilus	–	+	+	+++	55
Saccharomyces cerevisiae	–	+++ yellow	+++	–	30
Aspergillus niger	–	+++ green fuzzy centre	++	+	20–25

FIGURE 8.4
Part of the results section of the same microbiology lab report by Kavita Patel. The observations are presented in table format for easy comparison and effective organization.

Tables

Use a table when the precise numbers—including decimal places—are important. Tables allow your reader to scan and compare columns of numbers quickly. Arrange your table so the numbers are read down the columns and not across the cells. In Figure 8.4, Patel has placed observational data from a microbiology experiment in a table to help readers quickly compare the microbes.

Charts

Use charts to display data that show a trend or relationship. Provide a caption and title for each figure or chart. Convention dictates that you label the axes with the dependent variable (the one that you measured) on the vertical axis and the independent variable (the one that you manipulated) on the horizontal axis.

Diagrams and illustrations

Use diagrams or illustrations to present data that are not numerical. If appropriate, include the magnification of the image. Make sure that you include a number and caption with the figure.

Verbally Describe Your Results

Even though you have presented your data in tables, worked examples, diagrams, or charts, the results section should also include a textual description of the data. This does not mean that you repeat the specific numbers in words but rather that you provide a verbal overview of the various data you present, pointing out general trends and important features. Think of this verbal overview as a tour guide's commentary on the numbers. If you don't direct your readers' attention

Incorporating Visual Aids into a Lab Report

For a lab report that you are working on, identify four or five different groups of data that could be illustrated in a lab report. Decide on the best methods for representing each group, and develop the visualization for each one. Write a paragraph for each one, assessing how well you think the form suits the data and how effectively you think it makes the point that you want to make about that data. In your evaluation, be sure to explain what you think makes that choice effective.

DISCUSSION

The published optimal pH and temperature values for the micro-organisms in this experiment are as follows:

Table 5. Published Optimum Temperature Values for Micro-organisms

Organism	Optimal Growth Temperature (°C)
S. aureus	37
S. marcescens	12–36 (for red pigment)
P. fluorescens	4
B. stearothermophilus	55
S. cerevisiae	28–35
A. niger	25–30

Table 6. Published Optimal pH Values for Micro-organisms

Organism	Optimal pH
S. cerevisiae	4.5–6.5
E. coli	6.0–7.0
L. plantarum	5.5–5.8
S. aureus	4.5–6.5

Staphylococcus aureus has a published optimal growth temperature of 37°C, which is what was found in the experiment (*Staphylococcus aureus*, 2001). The bacteria have a published optimal pH of 4.5 to 6.5 (*Staphylococcus aureus*, 2001). This makes sense because *S. aureus* is bacteria that reside mainly in the human respiratory tract and on human skin, which have a near neutral pH and are maintained around the normal human body temperature of 37°C (*Staphylococcus aureus*, 2001). The bacteria can also be found in cows, chickens, pigs, turkeys, and unpasteurized food (*Staphylococcus aureus*, 2001). *S. aureus* does not compete well with other bacteria and is consequently found more often on cooked food than raw food (*Staphylococcus aureus*, 2001). *S. aureus* is normally a yellow color, so both the colony grown at 20–25°C and the colony grown at 37°C should have been yellow (*Staphylococcus aureus*, 2001).

Serratia marcescens grew best at 20–25°C. The published range for optimum growth and pigment production agrees with this result (Rafii, 1999). The red pigment is a combination of prodigiosin and pyrimine, which are produced by the bacteria in this temperature range when they are grown on peptone-glycerol agar aerobically (Rafii, 1999). *S. marcescens* only produces this pigment when grown under the correct conditions (Rafii, 1999). *S. marcescens* are found in soil, air, water, plants, and animals (Rafii, 1999). In the food industry, the bacteria have been found in milk, ice cream, coffee, fruit juices, eggs, and meats (Rafii, 1999). These bacteria are involved in opportunistic human infections as well as in food spoilage (Rafii, 1999). The experimental results agree with the published information about *S. marcescens*....

FIGURE 8.5
Part of the discussion section from Patel's microbiology lab report.

to what you believe are the key points, you miss an opportunity to prepare your readers for the interpretation of the results that you will make in the next section. They may well pay attention to quite different aspects of your data than you had intended, resulting in their resistance to the argument you present in the discussion. Note that, in Figure 8.5, Patel summarizes the data under each table, drawing readers' attention to her major insights about each data grouping. These summaries are helpful in directing the reader toward your broader conclusions about the data, which follow in the next section of your report.

Remember to confine yourself to presenting the data in the results section. Avoid getting into the interpretation that should rightfully appear in the following section, the "Discussion." At the same time, if you find yourself adding details about the procedure or materials, move them to the appropriate and previous section.

DISCUSSION

The discussion should follow from the information presented to this point. It should not restate your results; instead, make clear to your reader what the results mean and why they are important. In other words, explain the significance of your results and findings.

Remember how in the introduction you described the problem or reason for conducting this experiment? In this section of the report, you return to this point and explain how the work that you have done illuminates our understanding of the original problem. If your results contradict the findings of other published reports, say so, and try to explain what you think accounts for your different results. If your results are consistent with earlier studies, then you can point this out and underscore the importance of this agreement in results.

If there are broader implications for your results, then explore those in your discussion as well. If appropriate, bring in established theory or principles that help explain your findings. You can also suggest other experiments that need to be done or could be done, based on your findings from this one.

Conclude with a clear, concise summary of your conclusions and the main evidence upon which they are based. This summary gives you the opportunity to recap for your reader the main points that you want them to take away.

In Patel's discussion of her results (see Figure 8.5), she presents her key findings—the optimal temperature and pH values for the micro-organisms that she studied—in a table, so readers can quickly scan and compare the values from one strain of micro-organism to another and assess the accuracy of her measurements. In the textual discussion following the tables, Patel integrates established findings for this type of experiment with her own results to show their validity as well as to explain their significance.

REFERENCES

Use the style sheet for your discipline in preparing your references for the report (see Figure 8.6 for Patel's references). You may also find that the conventions for formatting references change from class to class. Be sure to find out (in advance, if possible) what is considered the acceptable format in each class. Usually the references are listed in alphabetical order. They generally include the following information, but the order and method of presentation can vary widely, depending upon the citation style being used:

For a Book

Authors' initials and last name, book title, publisher, city, and the year of publication.

For an Article

Authors' initials and last name, article title, journal title in which it appeared, volume and issue number, year of publication, and page numbers.

For Websites

Give as much information as you can, including authors' initials and last name, date that the file was created or modified, the title of the page and/or the title of the site.

If the reference is associated with an organization, include its name in the reference. Also include the date when you accessed the reference and the complete URL.

Do not use footnotes in a lab report.

Some libraries have purchased citation software that helps you format your references properly. Check with your school's library to find out whether you can gain access to software such as RefWorks to help you put your references section together correctly.

REFERENCES

Batt C. 1999. *Lactobacillus*. In: Encyclopedia of Food Microbiology. San Diego (CA): Academic Press. p. 890.

Cousin MA. 1999. *Pseudomonas*. In: Encyclopedia of Food Microbiology. San Diego (CA): Academic Press. p. 1290.

Department of Biology. 2004. Biology 140L: Fundamentals of Microbiology Laboratory Manual. Waterloo (ON): University of Waterloo. p. 77–81.

Escherichia coli. May 2001. New Zealand Ministry of Health; [updated 2004 Oct 24; cited 2004 Nov 25]. http://www.nzfsa.govt.nz/science-technology/data-sheets/index.htm.

Kozekidou P. 1999. *Bacillus*. In: Encyclopedia of Food Microbiology. San Diego (CA): Academic Press. p. 110.

Madigan M., Martinko J., Parker J. 2003. Brock biology of micro-organisms. 10th ed. Upper Saddle River (NJ): Prentice Hall. 1088 p.

Radke-Mitchell LC, Sandine WE. 1986. Influence of temperature on associative growth of *Streptococcus thermophilus* and *Lactobacillus bulgaricus*. J Dairy Sci. 69:2558–2568.

FIGURE 8.6

A partial list of references from Patel's microbiology lab report formatted in Council of Science Editors (CSE) style.

REVISING A LAB REPORT TO IMPROVE ITS ARGUMENT

Revise a lab report that you've already written to improve its organization and the quality of its argument. Incorporate the suggestions in this chapter.

When you have finished rewriting the lab report, write a short memo report to your instructor detailing the ways in which you changed the original draft to take into account the advice in this chapter for improving your lab report.

WRITING A LAB REPORT

Using the data from your lab notebook for an experiment that you've recently conducted, write a lab report following the advice in this chapter to write a strong report of the experiment. Include several visuals, as appropriate to the subject matter of the experiment.

CHAPTER NINE

Technical Communication Online

Posting and accessing technical information online is commonplace. Many people, when faced with questions about how to use some equipment or solve a technical problem, search online to find solutions or instructions posted by other people in similar situations. A wealth of information, technical and otherwise, is immediately available online with a few keystrokes. Search engines such as Google and Yahoo! make available thousands of links to web pages, and YouTube provides multimedia information that is educational and/or entertaining. Many technical communication documents that used to be distributed in print form—manuals, reports, etc.—are now uploaded to the Internet, and users access them from there, downloading a copy as necessary or reading them on screen.

If you are preparing technical communication resources that will be accessed and used online, this chapter offers a few guidelines to ensure that your online materials are useful to and usable by your readers. When designing documents that readers download for immediate use or save for later reference, choose a format that will make them easily available. While Word documents may be the standard in business environments, this format has limited accessibility outside of business. Instead choose document formats that don't require readers to own costly, proprietary software to open. Design your files by using standard formatting that maintains the document structure across diverse platforms and applications. For example, style sheets allow you to indicate relationships among document sections so that your organizational structure translates across electronic devices.

USE STRUCTURED DOCUMENTATION

Organizing documents by applying style sheets to them is called structured documentation. Structured documentation enables the efficient and accurate movement of documents between computer platforms (Windows®, Apple®, UNIX®), applications (Word, Google Docs®), and devices (phones, tablets, laptops). Style sheets allow writers to standardize how a document's structure is represented in an electronic file so that it can be shared. Not only can it be shared, but such documents can move seamlessly through hardware and software updates, minimizing disruption and wasted effort needed to reformat them with the new equipment or program. Most organizations have moved to structured documentation to maintain continuity as they upgrade their systems. Software style sheets accomplish two goals:

- Emphasize the organizational structure of the document
- Facilitate transferring the document from one program to another

Writers use a style sheet to assign specific formats to different aspects of the document or file, such as major and subordinate headings, ordered and unordered lists, or typeface changes. When you use style sheets to format your document, it forces you to first articulate the document's organization to yourself and then reveal this organization as you write the document. Your use and formatting of headings, tables, bold and italic fonts, and numbered sections then make clear to your reader the organizational structure of the document. For example, when you have to decide what level of heading applies to a particular section, your choice signals to the reader important information about the relationship between this section and the document as a whole.

When all of the organizational features of a document are coded with a particular formatting, the document can be transferred into a different program or program version, and the style sheet application will ensure that all formatting and design are preserved. What this discussion of structured documentation means for you as a potential employee is that you should make yourself proficient in the use of style sheets, whether for word processing or web design.

CONVERTING DOCUMENTS TO PORTABLE DOCUMENT FILE (PDF) FORMAT

One of the issues associated with transferring document files around an organization is the potential for changing or editing the draft. When multiple writers collaborate on a document, having each contribute her or his share is a good thing. However, when you need to distribute a document that you don't want changed or edited, a useful solution is to convert the file to a PDF, or portable document file.

Many organizations have found PDFs to be extremely useful for distributing technical and company documents. For example, a software engineer at a robotics company notes that he creates products and then documents them in PDF files that clients can download from the company website. This publishing of instructional technical documents online allows customers to quickly and easily locate updated documentation, which they can then read on screen or print off the pages that they need to use. Similarly, PDF documents can be opened by most users on diverse devices without having to purchase costly software.

SHARING DOCUMENTS ELECTRONICALLY

There are a variety of ways to share documents electronically. You are likely familiar with email attachments, which allow you to send word-processing files or images with an email message. Documents sent as email attachments represent the fastest and easiest way to disseminate information or projects around a company. One problem with sending email documents, however, is the potential incompatibility of the senders' and recipients' operating platforms or word-processing software. For example, documents composed on a Mac and written using some word-processing programs will sometimes not open with a PC. Files converted to PDFs can be opened and read by most recipients.

Google Docs offers an alternative method of sharing documents, especially if a group is drafting a document collaboratively. You can limit whom you share the document with, or you can elect to share it with whoever finds it. The interface and editing tools resemble those of most other popular editing programs. Recent versions of Word also allow users to share documents.

SHARED FOLDERS AND DOCUMENTS POSTED ONLINE

A growing trend in many organizations is to make documents available online and in shared folders on the company intranet. When documents are posted in shared folders on a server, people at different locations can help draft documents by accessing the files from the folders, adding information based on their areas of expertise, and then reposting the updated file for others to work on. This technology streamlines the collaborative process and contributes to overall productivity in significant ways. An advantage to using files in shared folders is that access to the files can be controlled. Document owners set permissions on the shared folders to control who can access the files and who can make changes. Usually, shared folders are only available to the individuals authorized to work on the particular files stored there, and employees must enter their identification information into the system to access these files.

Posting a Downloadable File Online

Share via Dropbox® or Google Drive®:

1. Create a PDF version of a file that you are willing to share.
2. Upload that file to Google Drive or Dropbox (free accounts are available for both) (see Figure 9.1 below).
3. Share your file with others: 👤+

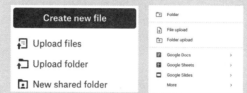

FIGURE 9.1
Upload links in Dropbox (left) and Google Drive (right). ©2018 Google LLC, used with permission. Google and the Google logo are registered trademarks of Google LLC.

You can also share documents through social media. LinkedIn and Facebook both offer websites through which you can share files by uploading them to your pages there. Another way to share documents is through your own website. By having your own website, you gain control over the way it is designed and displayed, and you also control how information gathered on your pages is shared.

One highly recommended site for doing this is called Weebly®. In Weebly:

1. Select "edit your site."
2. Click on "Build" and then click on the page where you want the link to download the file to appear.
3. Select "File" and drag the icon onto your page.
4. Click on "Click here to upload file" and fill in the dialogue box that appears to upload your file.

On LinkedIn:

1. Select "Me" on the menu bar at the top of the page.
2. Select "Posts and Activity" from the dialogue box.
3. Select "Documents" from the box at the top of the page listing posts, articles, and documents.

On Facebook:

1. Convert your PDF file to a JPG format.
2. Post the JPG file as a picture.

If you are working on a Facebook business or group page, click on "Post" and then "More" to see the option for adding a file.

CREATING AN ELECTRONIC PORTFOLIO

One way to use this electronic file-sharing technology as a student or practicing professional is to create a portfolio of your technical communication projects that may be accessed online. You may decide to save all of your completed work as a series of PDF files so that you and potential clients have easy access to past projects, or you might choose to design a special portfolio that presents sections of various exemplary projects. Adobe Acrobat® contains an option for creating a PDF portfolio that you might find useful. Of course, you can have print and online versions of your portfolio. If you print out your documents and put them into a binder, you have a portable record of your work that you can take to display and discuss at job interviews.

Depending upon the type of work you would like to do and the type of skills you have developed, you should post examples of your work that demonstrate the breadth and depth of your abilities. Some of the examples should be print, and others should be online documents, since technical communicators can be required to work in a variety of media.

If you decide to put together an electronic portfolio, you can probably post it on the personal website allotted to you by your educational institution or by your Internet provider. Consider also creating a website of your own through Weebly or WordPress® or another web-hosting service so that you have control over your content. Take a hard, critical look at the homepage to which you link your job application materials (including your electronic portfolio), and assess the site for its professionalism. When you send potential employers to your site, you want to make sure that they get a favorable first impression based on your website. If you have personalized your website to the point that it presents too much humorous, casual, or private, non-professional information, consider creating a second website for your professional development materials, so you *can* safely distribute that site's URL to potential employers. The goals of a personal website are usually very different and not necessarily compatible with the goals of a professional or job-search website.

WRITING AND DIGITAL MEDIA: ONLINE DOCUMENTS, VIDEO, SCREENCASTS, AND PODCASTS

Digital technologies have paved the way for technical documentation that is inexpensive to distribute and easily and cheaply updated. Digital versions of documents, whether manuals, assembly instructions, or resumes, can be accessed from anywhere in the world if readers have the appropriate technology. Given these facts, more and more organizations prepare technical documents that may be viewed exclusively online or downloaded and printed off. Others develop multimedia support documents intended to be viewed on a screen.

These digital documents, which are intended to be viewed and used on screen, are formatted differently than the documents made available for users to download and print. Online documents are designed to take best advantage of the screen format and of online capabilities, while downloadable documents linked to a web page are often adapted, print-friendly versions of their online counterparts. In this section, you will find information about the basics of structuring and developing web-based technical documentation. Good visual design and legible display largely determine how and what your online document communicates. Online documents are better understood as units of organized information, and the computer becomes a medium of communication or interface between users and the information. In this context, then, you can easily understand that your role as a communicator involves not only finding the right words but also packaging those words in chunks that correspond to the information needs of users.

From a technical communicators' perspective, online documents also present a number of advantages. You can improve your product quickly and cheaply, correcting errors and ambiguities as they come to light. You can update rapidly by posting new versions online that users can immediately access. It is also much less costly to upload a new digital version of an operations manual to a website than to print, bind, and distribute a new print edition of the same manual. Documents that are available online mean promoting a healthier environment, at least in terms of reduced paper production and recycling: hundreds or thousands of copies of print manuals that fairly rapidly go out of date do not need to be distributed (and often discarded) every year. Even if users are printing out copies of online manuals, they rarely print the whole volume; instead they print off the sections that they need.

ONLINE DOCUMENTS

While some of the principles that apply to creating usable print documents also apply to online documents, there are additional aspects to consider in planning and executing your online versions. These include organizing your information so that it is easily accessed using search functions, designing your layout to allow readers to easily understand where to look for the information they need, and writing that information in ways that assist users to read it.

Plan Your Document Navigation

As you know, a print book may be accessed by flipping through its pages: using this method, people can often stumble upon the information they need without consulting locating devices such as the index or table of contents. If they do use the table of contents or index, the page numbers help them quickly locate the specific section or page that they need. In contrast, users cannot "flip through" web pages, nor can they consult page numbers on a screen to be sure they have found the correct location of the information they need. Since users must use search functions or links to locate specific pieces of information, you have to plan your onscreen document thoroughly to ensure a clear and logical organization with plenty of visual and organizational cues to help direct users to the pages they need. Such cues include a clear, prominently placed navigation bar or menu on each page; a site map, which illustrates the overall organization of the document, and perhaps a site map link (on each page); and (if you have programming skills or technical support) a search function that allows users to search the site for the particular information they need. (Note: you can also add a search function to a website if you agree to the terms of various search engines, e.g., Google or Yahoo!. See https://support.google.com/customsearch/answer/4513751?hl=en&ref_topic=4513742 for an example of how to add a search function.)

Use Consistent Design Throughout

Develop your design for the website or online document, and maintain the design throughout. Use consistency of design as a signal to readers about where to look for particular information, as well as a means for them to understand what they are looking at and make sense of it when first viewing a page. If you locate navigational systems in the same place on the page, with the same design for buttons and labels, then users will quickly learn to look there and recognize the links they need to move around your website. If you use the same size and font choice for headings of equal importance, you can convey at a glance the relationship between major sections and subsections.

Be Succinct

Jakob Nielsen, an early usability researcher, based his command to be succinct (that is, brief and concise) on the fact that reading from computer screens is 25 per cent slower than reading from paper. Consequently, you should write 50 per cent less than you would if you were preparing the same information for a paper-based document. For PDFs, which can be used as print or online, assume readers will read them on screen since, generally, any text written for screen reading is easy to read when printed.

Check the spelling in your document before you post it. If you have generated it in a web-design program (which may not have spellchecking capabilities), you can copy and paste the text into a word-processing program and run the spellcheck there. Even when you have corrected all the errors that show up, don't consider yourself finished until you copyedit the text as well. This is a final opportunity for you to catch sloppy language and to remove any extraneous words—to make the text as succinct as possible.

ADDRESS READERS DIRECTLY

Address your readers in the second person (i.e., you) rather than the third person (i.e., he or she). Using second person reduces the distance between you and your reader, resulting in a more comfortable learning situation for readers. Second person is also the most concise: you want to use the fewest words to convey the most information.

USE THE ACTIVE VOICE

"Active voice" is a grammatical term that refers to putting the noun that is "doing" the action described by the verb in the subject position of a sentence.

For example, "the dog chased the squirrel" uses the active voice because the "dog," the subject of the sentence, is doing the chasing of the "squirrel," which is the object of the action (the one being done to). The alternative is the passive voice (e.g., "The squirrel was chased by the dog"). In the passive voice, the receiver or object of the action appears in the subject position (i.e., the squirrel), and readers must delay understanding the whole sentence until they get to the end. (What is the squirrel doing? Oh, the squirrel is not the main actor in the sentence. It's the dog.) This delay creates inefficient communication of your meaning. Passive voice also adds extra words to the sentence, making it unnecessarily longer. More significantly, however, is that sometimes the passive voice allows people to write a sentence without any real actor, causing ambiguity and imprecision, i.e., "The squirrel was chased." Consider this instruction in the passive voice: "It should be noted that one of the labels listed by Word may be adapted if the desired label is not listed in the Product Number box, or custom labels may be created." Here is a revision that uses active voice: "If you cannot find the label you want listed in the Product Number box, create your own custom label or adapt one of those listed." Use the active voice because it is the most concise, direct, and unambiguous.

WRITE SIMPLE, ACTIVE SENTENCES OR IMPERATIVE SENTENCES

Simple sentences (e.g., subject + verb + object) written in the active voice are direct, short, and easy to understand. They don't contain clauses that add to the complexity of the ideas and the time required to process these ideas. When you are writing prose that will be read or used online, keep your sentences short and simple to compensate for the added difficulty of reading and processing online information.

Imperative sentences are phrased as commands: "Choose the design that you want to apply to your oral presentation." They address the reader directly, they contain directive statements intended to instruct the reader, and they are concise. When you need to address the user directly, especially in a tutorial or other type of teaching situation, use the imperative to communicate the users' next step clearly and concisely.

UNDER-PUNCTUATE

Although you still want to include capital letters at the start of sentences and periods at the end, usability researchers suggest that you can omit many of the commas that you might use in a print document. When read on screen, commas add additional visual interference for users to process but often do not clarify the sentence meaning. For this reason, you can leave out commas from a sentence that is otherwise clear. For example, a comma that separates an introductory element from the main part of the sentence can be omitted unless the sentence is unclear without it. Commas separating a "which" clause from the rest of the sentence can usually be omitted as well. Similarly, you can leave off the commas at the end of each item in a bulleted list since, on screen, they interfere with understanding rather than clarify.

AVOID WORD VARIETY

When you are writing text that will be read online, reuse the same words rather than varying your vocabulary. Since your goal is to produce clear and concise text, repeat keywords to ensure clear connections between sentences. The clearer and more concise your text is the quicker your users will be able to scan and understand it. In fact, readers skim onscreen documents rather than read text: the repetition of vocabulary assists by helping them to fill in the information around the repeated words. When you introduce a new word, they have to pause to determine whether it is a new concept or merely a synonym. If it turns out to be a synonym, they slowed their work for nothing, resulting in momentary confusion and, then, irritation.

Write for Scannability

Usability research shows that users do not read online text fully: they scan it, picking up keywords and phrases. Anything that seems extraneous, they skip. Knowing this, structure your information using two or even three levels of headings to help users assess the relevance of the section to their needs. Also, use headings that are informative and descriptive. Based on the heading that precedes it, users should be able to identify easily what the content of the section will be. Actually, they will make judgments about the content based on your headings, whether these are well written and descriptive or not. If the heading appears irrelevant, they will skip that section.

Avoid formatting long, uniform blocks of text. Use bulleted lists to highlight or emphasize specific points. If the order of the points is significant, use a numbered list. After you have formatted a bulleted list with your main points, add short paragraphs elaborating each one. The idea is to provide users with multiple levels of detail. If they find a relevant or interesting bullet point, they will look for further information about it.

Highlight keywords to emphasize them, but do not underline. Remember that underlining on web pages means clickable links; underlining text for emphasis will confuse and annoy users. Instead, use bolding or a contrasting font. However, assess whether your choice of emphasis might confuse some users as signaling a clickable link.

Name Titles and Headings Effectively

When you are writing topic headings (or even web page titles), keep in mind these points to increase the usability of your pages.

- Eliminate articles (i.e., "A," "An," and "The") from the start of titles because they interfere with users' scanning the page. Demonstrative pronouns ("this," "that," or "these") and indefinite pronouns ("some," "many," or "few") can also clutter up the start of your titles.
- Move the information-carrying terms to the start of headings and titles so that key information reaches the reader quickly. For

example, revise a title that says "A Lecture on Web Usability" to read "Web Usability: Strategies and Guidelines."

- Give each page a different title that describes content.

Use Standard Web-Design Conventions

Web-design conventions are your friend. Use them because visitors to your site will expect to use your site the way they use other sites. Conventional site design allows users to understand navigational issues quickly and easily: if you subvert the conventions, for example by not underlining clickable links, then users will be momentarily confused about which elements on the page are links and which are not.

In *Don't Make Me Think!* (an excellent book on web usability), Steve Krug explains why you want to design a website or online document that is clear and obvious: "every question mark adds to our cognitive workload [as users], distracting our attention from the task at hand. The distractions may be slight but they add up, and sometimes it doesn't take much to throw us. As a rule, people don't *like* to puzzle over how to do things. The fact that people who built the site didn't care enough to make things obvious—and easy—can erode our confidence in the site and its publishers."[1] To maintain your users' confidence in your ability as a technical communicator, use Internet conventions in your site or document design so that users can focus on the information that you are presenting and not on how to use the site.

WHAT ARE THE CONVENTIONS?

- Underlined text is a clickable link.
- Blue underlined text is an active link.
- Purple or red underlined text is a previously visited link.
- Use high-contrast colors for text and backgrounds.
- Use plain or very subtle background patterns.
- Never use all caps anywhere on the page.
- Left-align almost all text.
- Use sans-serif fonts for body text.
- Make it obvious what is a clickable link.
- If you use animations or music clips, have them cycle twice and stop.
- Make both buttons and explanatory text into links.
- Use vertical, left-aligned lists of links rather than centered or right-aligned ones.
- Use moderate line lengths (i.e., 40 to 60 characters maximum for text blocks).

Since device screens are lit from behind, extended viewing causes eye strain. Some color combinations can make this eye strain worse. To minimize the strain on users' eyes, choose color combinations that have maximum contrast between

1 Steve Krug, *Don't Make Me Think!: A Common Sense Approach to Web Usability* (Berkeley, CA: New Riders Press, 2000), 140.

the background and the text. For example, combinations such as black and white or a very light color and a very dark color offer the most contrast. When adding a background to your document or webpage, choose solid color backgrounds for maximum legibility and contrast. If a textured or patterned background is essential, make it subtle enough that any text placed on top is still easily legible. To increase accessibility of your documents, files and webpages, include descriptions of the content of visuals, transcripts for videos, and ensure that the link destination is clearly presented in the text that highlights the link. Edit PDF documents to improve their accessibility by people using screen readers. If you are presenting your links in a column or list, left-align the list rather than centering or right-aligning it, especially if your audience is largely English-speaking. English (and other European) language readers automatically look left to find the beginning of meaningful visual and written communication. Capitalize on this impulse by placing your links where users will look: they will quickly find what they are searching for and therefore be more likely to use and appreciate your site. Make sure that your website is as clear and usable as you can make it for the widest possible audience.

VIDEO AND SCREENCASTS

2 Statistics for YouTube are taken from "YouTube for Press," YouTube, accessed February 28, 2020, https://www.youtube.com/about/press/.

YouTube has over two billion users.[2] Every day users watch over one billion hours of video. To reach audiences for your technical communication projects, consider creating videos to augment the documents you prepare. Think about what content in a document or on a web page should be written and what parts of the content could be conveyed through a video or a screencast (voice-over slide presentation).

Screencast vs. Text

A traditional way to teach about cohesion is through textual explanations (see Chapter 4, "Writing Technical Prose"). However, voice-over screencasts offer a new option.

Both have their places. The textbook explanation is in more depth, and reading about it creates an opportunity to think more slowly about the concept of cohesion. When it comes to putting the concept of cohesion into practice, though, the screencast provides both voice and slides that take viewers quickly into an explanation of how, exactly, they should revise.

FIGURE 9.2
This short video is an example of how to use a screencast to add voice to slide presentations.
Source: "Academic Writing Advice," Wecanwrite.ca, https://www.wecanwrite.ca/advice.html.

Create a Video/Screencast

The process of putting together video need not be complicated. Create slides as you would (or maybe already have done) for an in-person presentation. Record your voice using an application such as Screencast-o-matic® (https://screencast-o-matic.com/). Export the resulting file to YouTube or another video hosting service.

The key to effective videos is to keep them short. If your topic is more complicated, break it up into shorter chunks, aiming for one or two minutes. The shorter length keeps the files small and allows viewers to quickly find the section of the video they want to see. Keep in mind that viewers may watch the video several times; keeping it short helps them skip to the part they need to see again.

PODCASTS

Podcasts have emerged as another important mode for communicating technical information. As of March 2020, over 900,000 podcasts (think of a podcast as the equivalent of a TV show) were available. All of these shows have produced a total of over 28 million episodes. In short, many people use this mode of communication, with over 50 per cent of the US population listening to podcasts, and almost one-third listening every month.[3] Teaching Writing, a podcast by the authors, has had over 20,000 listens in two years.

3 "2019 Podcast Statistics, Demographics & Habits (US, Canada & Australia)," PodcastHosting.org, accessed March 29, 2019, https://podcasthosting.org/podcast-statistics/.

Podcast vs. Text

Just as videos and documents (see Chapter 4, "Writing Technical Prose") can convey technical information about how to revise for cohesion, podcasts can also be used to convey these ideas.

Podcasts can be supplemented with visuals, for example, slides (https://www.wecanwrite.ca/handouts-from-workshops.html) posted on a website, but much of their value comes from two factors:

- the files are tiny and can easily be downloaded onto a mobile device
- podcast episodes are listened to, and that enables people to do other things while listening

Ultimately, podcasts give technical communicators another increasingly popular way to reach audiences.

FIGURE 9.3
This podcast episode provides an example of another way to provide technical explanations.
Source: "Clear and Concise," Teaching Writing: Ideas and Strategies, https://www.podomatic.com/podcasts/rogergraves/episodes/2019-10-29T09_54_06-07_00.

Create a Podcast

To create a podcast, you need a host such as Podomatic® (www.podomatic.com).

The host site provides a place on the Internet for the podcast to live. The site walks you through the process of assembling the files you need, which include an audio file and a graphics file with cover art, and prompts you to provide information required for registering and posting your episodes.

You should write a script for each episode. Scripts typically include some kind of interesting opening, the main section that the episode is about, and then a conclusion in which you end the podcast and direct listeners to where they can follow-up with you or find more information.

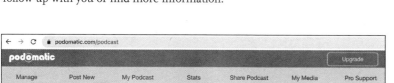

FIGURE 9.4
A screen shot of the Podomatic user interface.

You then need to record the episode and edit the file to remove stutters and any background noises. Audacity® (https://www.audacityteam.org/) is a great, free, open-source and cross-platform sound-editing application that is relatively easy to learn to use.

Once you have the sound recording exported to an mp3 or similar file, you must create cover art to help listeners find your podcast and your episodes.

The final step is to publicize the podcast. If there is a marketing or communications specialist in your organization, work with them to find ways to get the news out.

MAJOR PROJECT 9.1

PREPARING INSTRUCTIONAL MATERIAL FOR ONLINE DELIVERY

1. Write a set of instructions that users will access online.
2. Use the discussion in this chapter to help you design an effective layout.
3. Add illustrations to support the written text of your instructions.
4. When you have completed a draft of your online instructions, user test the site with at least three people from your target user group to help you decide how best to revise and improve your design and instructions.
5. Using the results of your usability test, revise the website.
6. Upload the final version to your course LMS or wherever your instructor has requested. If your assignment is posted somewhere other than your course LMS, email your instructor with the link to it.

CHAPTER TEN

Presenting Technical Information Orally

As veteran technical communicators, speaking opportunities will likely often be presented to you in your future careers. Your success in life will, to some degree, depend on whether you take these opportunities to speak publicly. Speaking opportunities can be personal (for example, wedding toasts in front of a hundred guests or eulogies at funerals), and professional (for example, formal presentations to company executives or hundreds of listeners, informal introductions of yourself and formal ones of someone else to small and large groups, and informal presentations to groups of co-workers).

The point is that you will make more of your career and your social life if you become comfortable speaking in front of a group. In this chapter, we offer some guidelines for getting started on what will likely be your lifetime of speaking publicly. Our goal is not to turn you into a politician. Our goal is that, when an opportunity to speak about your work publicly comes up, you will have some confidence that you can do so competently.

COMMON SPEAKING OCCASIONS

What kinds of speaking situations are you likely to find yourself confronting as a technical communicator? Speaking opportunities come in a wide variety of forms, ranging from

- casual, impromptu, short talks to small group meetings (3 to 7 people who know each other well);
- more formal speaking to small group meetings (3 to 7 people who hold various positions within the employment hierarchy or who are from outside the organization or your immediate work unit);
- informal, prepared presentations (to groups of 10 to 15 people within an organization);
- formal presentations (to groups of 10 to 15 people that include people outside the organization).

There are, of course, other presentations that you may find yourself doing: presenting recognition awards, receiving recognition awards, introducing yourself at meetings of your workgroup, or performing skits as part of a planning "retreat" or meeting away from the workplace.

FIGURE 10.1
Common speaking occasions.

CASUAL, IMPROMPTU, SHORT TALKS

These are the kinds of opportunities to speak that come up in the course of your everyday work. From time to time, you will need to meet with your supervisor, the other people in your workgroup, or as part of a cross-functional work team. Sometimes, these are just short meetings to find out how a project is proceeding; sometimes, groups of workers need to meet to go over policy changes in the workplace, e.g., to consider new health and safety procedures. You may be asked to give a short (30–60 second) update on the progress you've made documenting a section of a manual, for example.

How do you prepare for an impromptu talk, something that by its very definition is not scheduled? The real answer is that no one expects a polished, rehearsed performance in this kind of situation. Instead, they expect you to have and communicate some sense of how things are going on the projects you've been working on. Before you go to these kinds of meetings, take a few moments to review the status of each of the projects you are working on. Are they on time? Where are you in the overall development schedule for each one? Is work proceeding smoothly, or are there some challenges you face? How can you phrase these challenges diplomatically? If you take a few minutes to prepare your thoughts in advance, you can respond with confidence (and clarity) if/when asked about your work progress.

When you meet with cross-functional teams, the other members may have only a sketchy idea of what you do. Prepare a 30-second sound bite that summarizes what you do or some key aspect of your work. If you are working on usability testing of documents or a website, prepare a brief overview of what this involves and have it ready when you meet with groups who are unfamiliar with your work.

In some cases, the leader of a group may inform members about a pending change in how things are done at your workplace; then, he or she may ask how that change affects you. Although there is no way to prepare for this specifically, your answer will probably make more sense if you have up-to-date knowledge of where you are in your work.

FIGURE 10.2
Small group presentations.

SPEAKING TO SMALL GROUP MEETINGS

These meetings tend to be called for a reason or to get some work done. To that end, you may be asked to prepare a document or other materials to present to the group. When you meet with the group, you may distribute copies of the document or materials before you speak (perhaps by sharing a link to a Google document or slide deck), while you are speaking, or after you speak.

The key difference between these kinds of speaking opportunities and short, impromptu speeches is preparation. If you are giving a status report for a project you are working on, consider preparing a draft of the report in memo form to distribute at the meeting. You could use this as the basis for your comments and summarize the main points for readers as they skim the document.

Alternatively, consider preparing a short handout (one or two pages) that is an example or draft of one section of the manual or document you are working on. This handout will enable the other members of the group to visualize what you are working on and what it will look like when it is finished. From the small sample section that you give them, they can extrapolate what the rest of the project will look like.

INFORMAL, PREPARED PRESENTATIONS

These are similar to small group presentations but differ in degree: you are the focus for a few minutes, and the point of your remarks is to generate discussion. The meeting itself may still be an informal gathering of team members or committee members who all know each other, but your contribution to the gathering functions to focus or jump-start discussion. The gathering itself may be informal, but your part still needs to be prepared.

In a small group presentation, you could distribute a handout, such as a photocopy of a sample document, and it would be readily accepted. When you have been asked specifically to speak to some issue at some length (over two or three minutes), you should prepare a more thorough presentation. In this case, determine what you have been asked to do:

- Prepare an overview (for example, of a specific technology)
- Give background or history of a project
- Present two alternative plans of action
- Summarize a policy or procedure currently in place or that is being proposed

IN-CLASS EXERCISE 10.3

Delivering a Short Oral Report

Prepare a short, one- to two-minute progress report on an assign- ment or project that you are working on in your technical communica- tion class (or another class) to deliver orally to a small group (five to six students) in the class. Form the group around small tables, sitting so that you face each other. Bring copies of your proposal or just the overview or outline of your proposal so that the other members of the group can get a sense of the scope of your project while they are listening to you.

Check with your supervisor to find out how much time will be allotted to discuss- ing this issue and how much of that time should be spent with you talking.

Once you have a sense of the scope of the topic and of the time that will be given to it, prepare a point-form outline of what you want to say. You could use presentation software to prepare this and then distribute just the photocopies of the slides without formally showing the presentation itself. The slide handouts would provide some structure for your remarks and would show that you took some time to think about the topic. Use this part of the preparation process to think of the overall direction and message that you want to convey to the people in the meeting.

Once you have a general sense of the main points you want to convey, decide if you need to provide your audience with more detailed information. Do people need the full text of your remarks written out? Do they need a copy of the notes? Will you be referring to documents they have never seen or will need to review later, after the session? These other ancillary materials should not take over your presentation; instead, you should consider making copies of them available at the meeting or upon request. (For example, you could email them or share a digital file later to whomever is interested.) The focus of your work here is to consider just how much information your audience needs to know at this point, at this meeting, and to provide it. By making supplementary information availa- ble through other means, you are reaching out to the various people within your audience, whose members have different levels of knowledge about or interest in your topic.

Sample assignment

3C. Synthesis of Research
For this assignment you are to write a research report on a scientific topic. Your job in this document is to synthesize the relevant knowledge on a specific area of research.

> The point of the assignment + the genre: research report

Task 1. Find a scientific topic. Do some research to obtain an overview of research in this area.

Task 2. Examine the existing evidence (find between 4 and 6 different sources), and synthesize them into a coherent overview of the research.

Task 3. Using the sources that you chose, write an 800-1000 word report in which you summarize the evidence on the topic. In your report show your readers how the research can be organized into a coherent overview of the topic. Your report should help readers follow your thinking and arrive at a similar conclusion to yours about this topic.

> Steps/process

FIGURE 10.3
Sample handout.

FORMAL PRESENTATIONS TO LARGE GROUPS

Moving from the small group to speaking in front of a larger group (15 people plus) represents a difference in kind, not simply in number. These larger groups behave differently: you can't quickly make eye contact with everyone in the group, for example. Several members of the group are likely to be distracted at any one time; if you happen to focus on those few people, you may be discouraged and thrown off by them even though the bulk of the audience is listening attentively. At some point in the presentation, someone may need to get up and leave; if this happens in a small group, that person usually offers an explanation. In a large group, however, the unspoken etiquette is to say nothing but to leave as unobtrusively as possible. As a speaker, though, you may begin to wonder why some people are leaving, whether anyone else will also be leaving, whether you are being boring, and any number of other thoughts. The result is that you may be distracted from what you are trying to communicate. So speaking in front of larger groups presents problems that are distinctly different from speaking to fewer people in less formal situations.

Most invitations to speak formally come well ahead of when you will actually give the presentation. Many organizations have quarterly group meetings or yearly sales meetings at which several people will be asked to speak to the entire group. Unless you have been asked to fill in for someone else, you will probably have at least a week and maybe several weeks or even months to prepare for this event. In a technical communication course, you may have been notified by the course syllabus that you will be giving a presentation to the class during the last week of term, a presentation based on your final project, for example. One of the keys to your success will be your ability to use your time well leading up to the presentation to prepare for it.

FIGURE 10.4
Formal speaking engagements.

The first step in preparing for any presentation involves identifying specific details of the engagement:

- How many people are expected to attend?
- Who, specifically, will be there? Your supervisor? Clients?
- Is this a mixed group with varying levels of knowledge or a group whose members share a common background?
- What is the venue? How large is the room? What does it look like?
- How will the room be set up? Rows of chairs? Tables?
- Can the lighting of the room be controlled to allow for presentation slides?
- Will you be able to set up whatever technology you need ahead of time? Can you use your own technology (e.g., laptop)?
- Is this primarily an information session or a presentation to a decision-making body?

You want to have answers to as many of these questions as possible while you prepare the presentation. Some of these questions dictate the materials you can use in your presentation. For example, if you have been asked to present on your writing as part of a job interview, you would want to know whether you will have access to the web to show examples of your work, say, from your electronic portfolio. Consider storing your presentation on a USB flash drive or the cloud and running it from the equipment in the room. Sometimes, the venue and its setup affect a speaker's preparation in other ways too. For example, you may need to stand still behind a microphone or podium, or you may need to move around, in certain circumstances, to be seen by all.

Although these material conditions are very important, equally important is getting to know who will be sitting in the seats listening to you. If these people are a homogenous group then you can make assumptions about what they know and what you don't need to explain as you begin your talk. However, if your group is drawn from a cross-section of employees, then you may not be able to assume as much about them, and you may have to focus more on explaining terms and concepts that will be new to many of your listeners. So one thing to discover is how much background knowledge the audience shares.

MAJOR PROJECT 10.1

CREATING AN ORAL PRESENTATION OF THE FINAL COURSE PROJECT

Create a three- to five-minute presentation for your classmates and instructor about some aspect of your final project in this course. Select a topic from or a perspective on your project that you think will interest the class, and create a presentation that includes a visual or a demonstration of a technique covered in the final project.

Another consideration has to do with decision making: are you giving a presentation to a decision-making group, or are you giving an information-rich presentation to a group that wants to learn about something you are working on? The difference is critical because decision-making audiences will be less tolerant of poor preparation, less willing to listen to information if they have not been told why they need to know it, and more likely to be thinking about the implications of what you are saying. They prefer a direct summary of your main points; consider preparing photocopied handouts that present fuller discussions of what you have to say. These they can read later or during the presentation itself. (For a sample handout, see Figure 10.5.) Of course, it takes time to prepare reports and handouts that elaborate or support some point you want to make, but that time will be well spent. You will be seen as not wasting the time of the committee or group sitting in front of you, and they will think well of you for that.

Information-based presentations tend to be less intense than decision-making presentations. Often, they are part of an overall sales, marketing, or service program. The focus in an information-based presentation is conveying information about the subject itself rather than attempting to finalize policy changes. The audiences for information-based presentations may be expecting you to inform them about the project you are working on. As you plan your presentation, think about what kinds of information should be presented in handouts, what kinds could be summarized in a presentation slide, and what kinds of information might best be demonstrated (perhaps by visiting a website, perhaps by distributing samples). You want your presentation to provide the overall organization of the talk, giving it coherence. In support of the points you want to make, you could show the audience examples (see Figures 10.3, 10.5, and 10.6), lead demonstrations of a particular technology, or engage the audience interactively in a discussion of the topic. These are all methods of informing them in an interesting way.

Style: A template for analysis

Words

Feature	% of passage in target text	% of passage in your text
Monosyllabic/polysyllabic		
Active/passive		
"To be" verbs (is, are, be)		
Concrete/familiar/colloquial/plain		
Conceptual/abstract/abstruse/embellished		

Sentences

Sentence type	% of passage in target text	% of passage in your text
Simple (subject + verb + other)		
Compound (simple sent. + [and/but/;] simple sent.)		

FIGURE 10.5
Handout distributed to audience.

Link sentences from start to start

"Various techniques have been used to deposit a film or coating on a substrate located in a vacuum chamber. One technique simply is to vaporize a metal thermally. Another technique is referred to as chemical vapour deposition . . ."

FIGURE 10.6
Presentation slide that shows an example.

GUIDELINES FOR PREPARING PRESENTATIONS

Whether you are giving an impromptu introduction of yourself or a 30-minute presentation to the management committee where you work, some basic guidelines will help you make a better impression.

DECIDE WHAT INFORMATION TO INCLUDE IN YOUR PRESENTATION SLIDES OR OUTLINE AND WHAT TO INCLUDE IN A HANDOUT

Presentation slides are good for short phrases and fewer than 20 words per slide. If you have more than this number of words, consider moving that information to a handout that you can photocopy and distribute to your audience to read. Similarly, if you have a chart or table of information that you want your listeners to review, decide whether they can digest the information in the table quickly. If it will take them more than a minute or so to review the table, consider providing a photocopy of it.

DETERMINE HOW MUCH BACKGROUND TO PRESENT EARLY IN THE PRESENTATION

If your listeners share a similar background in the topic you are speaking on, you should be easily able to determine what they already know. With that settled, you can quickly establish a starting point for your remarks. However, if audience members do not share a common knowledge level on your topic, provide a few slides that will help establish a common framework of understanding. In addition, provide a handout that summarizes any technical language you may be using or perhaps a graphic that gives an overview.

ORGANIZE YOUR PRESENTATION SO THAT LISTENERS CAN FOLLOW YOUR THOUGHTS

Provide clear cues (sometimes called *signposts*) to your listeners, so they know where you are in the presentation: "The *second* main area we worked on...." By providing an outline of your talk or copies of the slides you show, you can also help listeners understand where you are going with the presentation and how its different parts are related. Remember that your audience is listening, not reading, so they will find it more difficult to understand your presentation's overall organization. To compensate for this, stress the organization of your presentation, and make it obvious to your audience.

CREATE VISUALS TO ACCOMPANY YOUR VERBAL DESCRIPTIONS

Just as you should **not** read your presentation to the audience word for word, you should also create opportunities to communicate through visuals. When creating slides using presentation software, limit each slide to around 20 words and to three or four major points. Use a large font—28–32 points—and add graphics from clip art or images from screen captures or picture files to illustrate the points you are making.

GUIDELINES FOR CREATING SLIDES

In *slide:ology: The Art and Science of Creating Great Presentations*, Nancy Duarte outlines how to use presentation software such as PowerPoint, Prezi, or Keynote to support the message you want to convey in a presentation. In the introduction to this book, Duarte emphasizes that "presentation software is the first application broadly adopted by professionals that requires people to think visually."[1] The key point is that the slides you create must use visuals **AS WELL AS** words to communicate your message and that visuals must dominate the slides.

1 Nancy Duarte, *slide:ology: The Art and Science of Creating Great Presentations* (Sebastopol, CA: O'Reilly Media, 2008), xviii.

WHO IS YOUR AUDIENCE?

Work hard to describe the audience for your presentations. For a class presentation, who are the students in your class? Are they in the same major as you are? Why did they take this class? What are they interested in? Can you demonstrate some aspect of your topic that they are not familiar with but that might help them?

BRAINSTORM IDEAS FOR SLIDES

What points do you want to make in the presentation? Write them down, one at a time. Rearrange them into a structure, if one comes to mind.

TELL A STORY

Your presentation must tell a story: how you came up with your final report, why the project is ahead of schedule, how the program has developed in the last eight months.

CREATE YOUR SLIDES

1. Use visuals and words (fewer than 20 words per slide, preferably phrases and headings).
2. Highlight the conclusion or the point you want to make.
3. Simplify the slide, not the idea: explain the context and detail verbally, not on the slide.
4. Use contrasting elements (titles in a different font or color, for example) to lead the audience to your main point.
5. Use lists to show relationships between main ideas and subordinate ideas.
6. Use multiple slides rather than cramming details onto one slide.
7. Avoid sub-bullets: they are a sign that you have too much text on the slide.
8. Use color to highlight key ideas.
9. Use sans-serif fonts (Arial, Verdana, Helvetica).
10. Use a minimum of 24-point font; this will also keep your word count low.

Prezi: Overview and Zoom

Prezi (prezi.com) offers an interesting alternative to sequential slides. The big advantage of Prezi is that it allows you to communicate the overall structure of your presentation at a glance. Headings communicate major topics of discussion, and you can zoom in and go into detail in response to audience interest. You can also run a Prezi presentation along a predetermined path, much in the way that you would with a linear slide presentation.

Prezi is inherently visual, and it can be challenging to create a visual structure that functions as an overview that you use as a starting point for the presentation. Each area on the main display becomes a kind of sub-slide that you can zoom into. If the audience can't read the font, simply zoom in some more. This also controls how much they can read: they can only read what you zoom in on. You can embed as much information as you want—it remains invisible until you zoom in on it.

GUIDELINES FOR GIVING PRESENTATIONS

When it comes time to actually move to the front of the room, keep these guidelines in mind.

TAKE ADVANTAGE OF THE IMMEDIACY OF HAVING LIVE HUMAN BEINGS IN THE SAME ROOM WITH YOU

Although it is stressful to speak in front of people, audiences also offer energy because of the interaction between you and your listeners. People want you to **LOOK THEM IN THE EYE** rather than have you avoid their gaze. Identify a few people in the audience, and actually look at them as you speak. You don't have to look at every person in the room—in fact, it may not be possible—so long as you do make eye contact with some of the people in the audience.

Related to this advice about connecting with your audience is the level of vocabulary that you use when you speak; linguists call this "register." When speaking in a business setting, use the same level of language that you would use when in a meeting or on the phone with co-workers or customers. Avoid overly formal, stilted language ("I do believe that you are mistaken, Mr. Brown") in favor of the kind of language you would actually use if you were sitting down at a small meeting with other co-workers from another part of the company.

STAND SO YOUR AUDIENCE CAN SEE THE VISUALS THAT YOU DISPLAY ON THE SCREEN

Stand off to one side of the screen on which you are displaying your visuals, so your audience can see them without having to look around you. One consequence of your standing to one side is that you will be less tempted to wander around the room. Your audience does not want to watch as you stride around the room and into the audience.

CONTROL THE TIMING OF THE SLIDES SO YOU CONTROL WHEN THE PRESENTATION MOVES FROM ONE TOPIC TO ANOTHER

The slides function as a kind of moving outline of the talk. As soon as a new slide appears, the audience will read it. Don't display the new slide until you want to move the conversation forward. This tactic allows you to take questions during the talk, provided you control when the slides advance from one to another.

BREATHE

It may seem obvious, but one way to make sure you get started well is to pause for a second or two to take a deep breath. Another tactic is to take a look around and say hello to someone you know in the audience before getting started formally. That will get the first words out of your mouth and clear your throat before you try to raise your voice and project it so that everyone in the room can hear you.

The key to a good presentation is preparation. If you prepare handouts and interesting slides, your audience will have something to look at other than you. They will sense that there is value in what you are about to say and encourage you to continue. That will help you get started, and once you get started you have a very good chance of finishing—and finishing well.

Index

From the Publisher

A name never says it all, but the word "Broadview" expresses a good deal
of the philosophy behind our company. We are open to a broad range of
academic approaches and political viewpoints. We pay attention to the
broad impact book publishing and book printing has in the wider world;
for some years now we have used 100% recycled paper for most titles.
Our publishing program is internationally oriented and broad-ranging.
Our individual titles often appeal to a broad readership too; many are
of interest as much to general readers as to academics and students.

Founded in 1985, Broadview remains a fully independent
company owned by its shareholders—not an imprint
or subsidiary of a larger multinational.

For the most accurate information on our books (including
information on pricing, editions, and formats) please
visit our website at www.broadviewpress.com. Our print
books and ebooks are available for sale on our site.

broadview press
www.broadviewpress.com

MIX
Paper from
responsible sources
FSC® C013916